St. Louis Writers Guild 100th Anniversary Members Anthology

Founded in 1920

ISBN: 9798612728801

St. Louis Writers Guild is 501©3 nonprofit organization with the mission to further Missouri's literary heritage, connect, support, and promote writers and literary organizations in the community.

St. Louis Writers Guild
Founded in 1920
A chapter of Missouri Writers Guild
@stlwritersguild #SLWG #YWSTL
stlwritersguild.org

Cover design by Brad R. Cook
Cover Photo from Pixabay.com
SLWG Logo (2015) by Brad R. Cook,
Steven Langhorst, and Jennifer Stolzer
Interior Layout by Brad R. Cook
Arch graphic from Pixabay.com

For

The Members of St. Louis Writers Guild

You have friends here!

St. Louis Writers Guild
100th Anniversary Members Anthology

Dearest Member,

As the new president of the St. Louis Writers Guild, I wanted to take a minute to thank you for all of your hard work. Your submissions to this member anthology are the true testament to how much our membership loves what they do and how much they support the Guild in our never-ending endeavor to promote literacy and community. Your support of the Guild means a lot to me and the other members of the board but your support of each other means more. This anthology was the Guild's attempt to connect members to each other and highlight the work we all give our souls to produce. Keep writing. Keep reading. Keep supporting.

You have friends here,

Jessica Mathews
President
St. Louis Writers Guild

Zing the Sting of Rejection

Linda O'Connell

The decorative, hand-woven basket on my desk is filled with writing contracts and publishing acceptances. There would be another basket equally filled with rejections— some formal, some standard, and some with personal editorial notations— **if** I collected rejections. But I deliberately discard or delete negativity when it arrives in my mailbox or my in-box. There's a larger wicker basket in my study, stuffed with hard copies of all my writing submissions, proof that I tried.

Disappointment happens to the seasoned writer as well as the novice. I have learned an effective technique to zing the sting that comes from receiving rejections— which still occur, twenty plus years after I began writing seriously.

As excited as a child on Christmas morning, I hurried to the computer to search for my name among the list of creative non-fiction writing contest winners. My shoulders slumped. I frowned and moaned. I did not take first, second, or third place. I read and reread the names of the ten honorable mentions, none of which were mine. My ego deflated, and I fought the urge to call myself a loser and compare myself to the prize winners.

I have always had a love of writing. When I was a young mom, and other stay at home mothers in the neighborhood watched and discussed Days of Our Lives, I chronicled the days of my childrens' lives in their journals when they napped.

I enrolled in a college composition writing class fifteen years after high school. The first day, I waited nervously for the professor and students to file in. I sat in an empty classroom for fifteen minutes before I realized I was in the correct room number, but the wrong building tower. I felt like a real loser walking in late, and I felt inferior to the younger students. By semester's end I felt validated. The professor's red ink comments boosted my self confidence.

"If I graded journals (personal essays) on a competitive basis, you would have the only consistent "A" in this class, and the next highest grade would be a C-." He encouraged, "Do something with your talent!"

I enrolled in an evening adult education writing course. The seasoned instructor hustled in shifting an armload of papers. She shocked me when she announced, "Everyone starts this class with excess fat. I'm going to show you some exercises so you can leave some of your weight on the floor."

"Not again!" My heart palpitated. I thought, "I'm in the wrong room. No way did I sign up for an exercise class!"

An older man leaned towards me and asked quietly if I had ever checked out the slicks. Did he mean hard bodies? Slick weight lifters? I was ready to walk out of the classroom when the instructor announced, "I am going to show you how to tighten things up."

Admittedly my thighs needed some work, but I wasn't there for weight loss. I shuffled my notebook and pens, slid my purse strap over my left shoulder and was ready to scoot out of my desk when the teacher said, "It will be difficult to slice and dice parts of your personal essays and leave pieces on the floor."

I sighed with relief, relaxed, and listened to her advice for the next eight weeks. I discovered "slicks" were magazines. I learned valuable writing lessons: writing is subjective, and nobody's writing pleases every reader. One message resonated, "Rejection is seldom about you, personally. It is as much about particular editorial needs."

I developed better coping skills and a positive attitude when I began submitting my work. I stopped considering myself a reject and realized the rejections were not personal. I admit, there have been times I've put my hands on my hips and stomped like the five year old who resides deep in my psyche and complained, "They don't know what they're missing!"

I learned not to wallow in pity or dark chocolate for too long, although I admit, I do devour a tiny square to quell my inner critic when she occasionally raises her head and gives me the side eye.

With a dose of eternal optimism, and realistic expectations, I return again and again to do what my heart calls me to do: write. There is a song in my soul that begins when I spill words onto paper. I delight in the formation of the perfect paragraph. It feels as though I'm writing a symphony. A rejection received is simply part of the orchestra: cymbals clanging, "not this time." Instead of despair, I cheer inwardly, knowing that my submission was read by at least one reader. I believe that if it is meant to be, my inspirational and/or humorous words will reach a greater audience and influence others. Then I get to work revising and recycling to another writer's market. To date, I have more than 250 writing credits in regional, national and international publications.

Negativity is a heavy and unnecessary burden to carry around. It can stop us in our writing tracks. Once we decide to delete self criticism, a weight is seemingly lifted, and it is easier to zing the sting of rejection and move forward.

For more, visit: lindaoconnell.blogspot.com

The Right Note

Ellen Parker

Nikki smoothed the symphony program against her best summer skirt. Voices murmured around her, punctuated with occasional soft laughter. The seats were filling. The orchestra would have a good crowd at their season finale.

She glanced at the empty seat to her left. Who had Cousin Julie given her ticket to? *The nice guy in the next cubicle.* Her relatives needed to get more original in their attempts to set her up on a date.

Five minutes to the first note. Nikki closed her eyes and conjured up an image of an accountant working with her cousin. Fat, bald, and thick glasses settled on a very ordinary, forgettable face. Tonight she would pay special attention to the music. *May the good Lord preserve me from well-meaning extended family.*

"Excuse me. Pardon me." A tall, slender man apologized to other guests as he moved down the row toward her. He eased past the last pair of knees, dropped into the seat, and extended his hand. "Joe Holmes."

She gulped down a cry of shock as the mental picture constructed with care exploded into colored smoke. Inspection from his alert blue eyes brought heat flashing up her neck. "Nikki James."

"Julie forgot to tell me her cousin was beautiful."

"What did she say?" Nikki forced

the handshake into brief and busied her hands with the program. She denied her fingers another excuse to touch him.

He kept his mouth in a straight line and gave a tiny shrug. "The ticket will put you next to my young cousin, an engineering student."

"Julie's a woman of few words." She began a list of items left off in the voice mail this afternoon. Blond. Young. Easy smile.

"Does it...?" The balance of his question was smothered by applause for the concert master.

Nikki divided her attention between the featured soloist and the man beside her during the first movement of the concerto. She watched the musician's fingers fly over the piano keyboard, climbing, crossing, and caressing notes from the instrument. Every few bars, she caught a glimpse of Joe's index finger tapping a silent accompaniment on his knee.

Don't stare. She forced her gaze from Joe's blunt, smooth nail to the pianist's face.

The final note of the first movement faded into space. Nikki jumped an inch off her seat at a touch on her shoulder.

Joe pointed to uneven words added to the margin of his program. "Do you play?"

She found her senses, plucked the offered pen from his hand and wrote. "Not serious."

"Two years piano—six clarinet." He finished in competition with the opening chord from the orchestra.

Twice before intermission Nikki found her glances at Joe intersected by his inspection of her. She brushed non-existent lint off her silk blouse and looked down to confirm that all the buttons were secure. Tomorrow she'd be calling Julie and telling her...telling her what? She'd found a gem? A pretty boy shell? Or...?

"Very nice." Joe leaned close and slid his words under the standing ovation for the pianist.

Nikki nodded and wondered what exactly he was

referring to. The music that had become background for her thoughts? The modern concert hall? Or the warm blush that persisted on her neck? "Do you attend often?"

"My goal is three times a season. Tonight's a bonus. Usual seat is over there." He pointed to the section beside the violins. "May reconsider in the fall."

"I like a clear view of the cellos. That was my instrument in high school." She blinked away an image of the last time she'd played—New Years Day.

"I hear you're from St. Louis, so I'll have to ask. Which high school?"

"Bishop DuBourg. My protestant parents sent me to neighborhood Catholic schools." Formal manners rubbed in by word and example from Nikki's mother won the moment and kept her smile polite and proper. "And you? I'd expect that query from only another St. Louis escapee?"

"Guilty as charged. Afton. Ran away to college in Kansas City and stayed."

"Running from family?"

"What else?" He smiled wide and brief. "They're so bad I've been trying to transfer to the St. Louis office for the past six months."

Nikki failed to prevent a genuine laugh from escaping. "Sounds like a page from my life."

The house lights dimmed for a moment, the signal for guests to return to their seats.

"Two quick questions before the music starts." Joe advanced his hand toward her arm and then retreated. "What sort of engineering? Will you have ice cream with me after the concert?"

She opened her mouth, but before a sound could cross her lips, the orchestra struck the first, perfect chord of a popular symphony. *Ice cream?* She risked a glance at his profile and sighed. Every word from her "date" struck the right note.

For more, visit:
ellenparkerwrites.wordpress.com

Blood Simple

Rick Skwiot

Previously published in St. Louis Magazine, July 2008

When I was a child we lived on a lake in rural Illinois outside Granite City where my father worked at a steel mill. But on weekends he was outdoors. In winter ice skating on the frozen lake or walking off across the shorn cornfields with his shotgun and hunting dog, searching for rabbit or quail. In summer, working in the garden, repairing the rustic house or fishing shirtless from our boat dock or from his homemade rowboat, gliding over the still lake. My mother, a blue-eyed, blonde granddaughter of northern German immigrants, would then caution him: "Put a shirt on, Ed. You're getting too dark."

Jim Crow in St. Louis

Although my father's parents came from Poland, he was not a round-faced, fair-haired Slav, but rather dark and wolfish, with olive skin that turned deep brown in the sun. My mother feared that when they visited friends or family across the Mississippi in segregated 1950s St. Louis, people would think she was with a "colored man" and abuse them for the transgression — "colored" then being the common public term for African-Americans, with St. Louis Post-Dispatch classified ad headings for apartments reading, "For Rent — Colored."

While my parents — and Jim Crow laws — have long since passed, my personal questions about race have persisted, for I inherited my father's strong facial features, dark skin and surname, in addition, seemingly, to his mercurial Slavic soul. This led me always to identify with my Polish heritage over my Germanic side and consider myself a Polish-American. Now, thanks to DNA testing, I've had to revise that designation — and my perceptions about race, ethnicity and culture.

My curiosity about my father's dark heritage was whetted by my parents' refusal even to entertain the question. "You don't need to know" was their usual response whenever I asked inappropriate questions about procreation and such, and they employed the phrase to end any debate or inquisition into our pre-American past as well. But in this case it was not out of embarrassment or delicacy, but likely out of ignorance and indifference.

Cass Avenue Poles

My father knew and cared little about his family's European past. To him it was a stigma best ignored, hidden or denied. Born in 1914 in the North St. Louis Polish community centered on Cass Avenue, he viewed his ethnicity as the social handicap it surely was in Anglo-centric St. Louis society, and for a while had Anglicized our surname to "Scott." Although Polish was his first language (he learned grammatically correct, slang-free English in the St. Louis Public Schools), he refused to teach me any of it: "Speak American," he'd say.

However, I frequently heard Polish spoken, as his mother, Mary, who had come to the States in 1910, spoke virtually no English, even until the day she died, 60 years later. As a result, she also was little able to quench my curiosity about family history. Though I do recall a story she once told me — likely with my father translating — about Cossacks (she had claimed) raiding her village when she was a girl. They came on horseback as she was sitting outside with a neighbor who clutched an infant son to her breast — that is, until a horseman lifted the child from her arms on the end of his saber.

My Polish grandfather, Joseph, whom I never knew, had come to the United States in 1892 and worked in steel mills in Scranton and Chicago before finally settling in St. Louis. From genealogical research that I once conducted in a vain attempt to unearth my genetic past, I learned that he came from the same small Polish town, Zawady, as my grandmother. However, he left Poland two decades before she did, when she was but two years old. When she did finally come to St. Louis, alone, they married within a few months. I suspect it was an arranged marriage of some sort, with him paying her passage over. Such was immigrant courtship and romance circa 1910.

So despite my genealogical research and thanks to my parents' lack of knowledge and/or interest in such issues, I still didn't have an answer to my question: What was I racially? Though nominally Polish-American and German-American, I knew that a large measure of other genetic material — seemingly not northern European — tinted the mix. I conjectured in my childhood memoir *Christmas at Long Lake* that we were "perhaps descendants of raiders from the east. Or of Gypsies … Or perhaps of the Neuri, militant Iranian nomads who inhabited eastern Poland in the fifth century B.C. and who, according to Herodotus, turned into wolves at certain times of the year."

What I didn't realize until I finally submitted to DNA testing was how significant my non-European genetic makeup was, how genetically insignificant my Polish heritage was and how wrong I had been my whole life thinking myself a Polish-American.

DNA and Bloody History

DNA (deoxyribonucleic acid) is a coiled molecule composed of chromosome cells that transmit genetic information from generation to generation in all living organisms — like a set of blueprints.

Segments along the length of a human DNA molecule form sets of genes that we all share, though individuals can inherit different forms of a given gene, making everyone genetically unique.

After making arrangements with a testing lab called AncestryByDNA, I was sent a test kit, which contained two plastic swabs that I used to scrape DNA samples from the inside of my cheek — this is painless — and then mailed back to the lab in Sarasota, Fla. The lab then analyzed my DNA markers and compared my genetic composition to major population groups around the globe.

The test results indicated that only some two-thirds of my DNA came from northern European sources, with the rest coming predominantly from south Asia — that is, India and the Middle East — with a couple of percentage points from southeastern Europe: Turkey, Greece or Italy.

According to historians, the most common way that such Indian DNA mixed into European populations came via the migration of the Roma, often referred to as Gypsies. Some believe they came into existence as a people a thousand years ago when Middle Eastern Muslim invaders conquered northern India and marched the Roma back to present-day Afghanistan and Iran as slaves. Other historians think they were low-caste Hindus recruited and sent west to battle encroaching Islamic armies.

In either case, the Roma remained in the Middle East until the 14th century, when they began moving into Europe. Their migration — from India to the Middle East, then through Turkey and Greece to Eastern Europe — suggests a genetic road map that parallels my DNA results.

Ever since their arrival in Europe some 700 years ago the Roma have found little warm welcome. They have been alternately shunned, enslaved or slaughtered. In the years after my Polish grandparents landed in America, the Nazis attempted a Gypsy genocide that may have cost half a million lives, some eastern European Communist regimes tried to eradicate the Gypsies through sterilization — as did Norway, until 1977 — and in the 1990s Germany deported tens of thousands of Gypsies.

Similarly, descendants of my Middle Eastern ancestors have not fared well since my grandparents came to the States. Foreign intervention, war and oppressive Islamic fundamentalism have beset Persia/Iran and Afghanistan, with somber results for many inhabitants. And we know what the 20th century meant to whatever Polish and German kin I may have had in those homelands: totalitarian oppression, saturation bombing, bloody battles, death camps, invasion and hunger.

A Fortunate Migration

There is no way for me to know or gauge the suffering of my ancestors — whether Indian, Persian, Slav, Turk or Teuton — or to assess what impact, if any, it has on my character or essence. But I do know one highly pertinent and pivotal fact of my ancestral history: On April 5, 1892, my grandfather Joseph Skwiot disembarked the SS Bremen in Baltimore and after some two decades working in American steel mills managed to afford to have a bride sent him from his hometown in Poland. As a result, I was born an American.

Whatever genetic connection I might have with Gypsies, Germans, Slavs or Persians plays little role in who I am compared to that one central fact of family history. Anyway, scientists say that we all share 99.9 percent of our DNA, regardless of our ethnicity, and can all be traced back to a common ancestor in Africa 200,000 years ago — which suggests that race is perhaps nothing more than a social construct.

But what matters profoundly is that I have had the good fortune to be born and raised in a functional society, one that has done a rather good job of sustaining me — feeding me, educating me and protecting me from foreign invaders, oppressive rule or theocracy. Conversely, my ancestors — either by force or flight — left communities that were significantly dysfunctional for them: low-caste Hindus in India, likely heretical Roma in Islamic lands and lower-class Poles and Germans in rigid European aristocracies where their rights and opportunities were severely circumscribed.

And I am glad they did. However sorry I am for their suffering, it has miniscule effect on me in relation to the safe and nurturing environment in which I find myself. The social mobility, material opportunity and safety offered in the United States compare favorably to most of the remaining world — a fact obvious to disadvantaged people everywhere. Which is why folks like my grandfather continue to flock here — legally or illegally and often at great expense and risk — from societies far less functional for them and their families.

I am also glad for the $670 worth of DNA testing I got. Not for its opening up new avenues of genealogical investigation and knowledge for me or for the possibility of finding famous or infamous kin, but for alerting me to how truly unimportant my genealogy is and how preposterous my lifelong self-perception as a Polish-American has been.

Assuming that my light-complexioned mother transmitted to me only northern European blood and accounted for roughly half my genetic makeup, then the darker portions came solely from my father. Which suggests that, genetically, he was likely more Roma and Persian than Pole. Thus my Polish-American designation was correct only in a minor cultural way — in that I descended in part from people who came here from Poland speaking Polish — and little more. Speaking no Polish and having never been to Poland, I am now forced to reconsider my ethnicity and its meaning, and find it fairly meaningless.

Whether I come from Europeans or Asians, from whores and horse thieves or popes and princesses, matters not. What does matter, I see, is that I have been granted a culture that nurtures all ranks of people rather than oppressing or enslaving them on dubious grounds of race, religion or class. I witness socially disadvantaged and/or politically oppressed people from Asia, the Middle East, Europe, Africa and the Western Hemisphere coming here and actuating themselves materially, intellectually and spiritually. The prostitute's granddaughter becomes a professor or priest; the steelworker's grandson writes books and magazine articles instead of performing mean physical labor for a bare subsistence.

So I am abandoning forever my hyphenated existence — my Polish-Americanism — and suggest for accuracy's sake that we all should. By jettisoning the Polish-, Irish-, African- or Mexican- prefixes, we indicate that we are a new race — not genetically speaking, but culturally, which is ultimately what counts.

For more visit: rickskwiot.com

The Fourth Treatment

T.W. Fendley

"Remember how your growing bones ached?" I tried to remember but maybe I was just too distracted. I'm a visual person and it was taking a lot of effort to keep from staring rudely at Jorge's leathery, wrinkled face. Tufts of coarse brown hair jutted over his dark eyes, which were almost hidden in the cavernous space beneath his bulging eyebrow ridge.

"That's not a trick question," he said. "You can remember if you try."

It was about seventy years ago when I went through puberty. Still, I could recall the knocks and bruises from being out-of-sync with my growing body. But bones aching? "Sorry, Mr. Jorge," I said, throwing my hands up and smiling.

"Just Jorge," he said for the second time.

I felt almost like a kid again and, comparatively, it wasn't far from the truth. At four hundred eleven years old, Jorge92A2020 was the only survivor of the first dozen longevity pioneers.

"Each time I've gotten a Treatment, it's been like starting puberty all over again," he said. "You can't know how you will transform, except that it won't be from child to adult."

I chafed at the familiarity of his tone. He spoke to me like I was his daughter instead of a professional. I couldn't complain, though, because he'd gotten me past

Security into the family waiting area with no questions asked. I guess that was one of the perks of being Jorge. Jorge got what Jorge wanted. I still wondered why he wanted me to interview him instead of one of the more famous reporters who'd hounded him, including some on our own staff.

We sat facing each other in a pale green booth that was big enough to seat four, his hands resting on the tabletop over the Renu Center's familiar Tree of Life insignia. The symbol was repeated on the blue-green doors to the Advanced Treatment room, its entwined double DNA helixes portrayed as a gnarled trunk with the ends of the ladders stylized into the tree's canopy. Jorge was wearing a loose wrap of the same aqua color.

"How old were you when you took the First Treatment?" I had to get him back on track.

"Only ninety-two, though it was considered quite old at the time." Large, protruding teeth flashed as he carefully enunciated each syllable.

I figured I would be twice that age before getting my First Treatment here, a leap in longevity due largely to Renu's annual screening process. Most of us used home monitors to do our own annual testing, then chose from among a handful of generic booster packages. Across the hall, I could see some of the pampered few who were wealthy enough for personalized boosters here at the Center.

"Before I had my First Treatment, I hadn't thought about puberty in years," he said. "Why would I have?"

I smiled, but didn't say anything. He was back on the puberty thing again.

"Funny how some things come back to you at times like that," he said. "Before I hit puberty the first time, I had a moment of perfect clarity when I realized I wasn't going to be a child anymore. I was like the mythical figure—Peter Pan, wasn't it?—who didn't want to grow up."

"I don't know that story," I said. "You were talking about the First Treatment?"

"Well, Andrea, that year I played like a little kid, riding my bicycle around and around the giant oak tree my dad used for a hoist to lift engines out of his trucks," Jorge continued, as if I hadn't spoken. "That was back when trucks still had rubber tires and dirt was dirt."

"You were twelve then?" I asked, hopefully sounding less perturbed at his digressions than I felt. I needed for this interview to go well. I checked the time again. Jorge's appointment was in thirty minutes and we were only to the First Treatment.

"Yes. That summer, I got my period. I grew four inches taller, and my breasts developed. Things were never the same after that."

"You were female until your Second Treatment, right?"

"Right. They thought they knew what the treatment would do to our bodies. Of course, they were wrong." Jorge shifted positions, his badly curved spine a poor fit in the booth despite its ergonomic cushioning.

He was certainly right about the physical changes. In my research for the interview, I'd been lucky to find one pixilated hologram that had somehow managed to escape deletion in the online wars. The wide-angle shot taken in front of Renu's Ogden Research Center showed all twelve who'd taken that historic First Treatment. I couldn't determine much about what Jorge actually looked like. Even so, I was unsettled by the comparison to how he looked now.

A doc-tech emerged from the blue-green doors, stopped near the glass wall that encircled the room and began arranging the injectors for Jorge's procedure.

"Anyway, I'd been a major investor in Renu from the beginning and closely followed the research, so I was the first to ensure myself a slot when the longevity treatment trials finally began. They said the Treatment would regenerate the body I had at forty," he said, "and that sounded good to me."

"It was everything you imagined it would be?"

"You have to realize, Andrea, this

had never been done before. The
quest for immortality had gone on for centuries, and no
one knew if we could truly reverse aging. It wasn't like
it is now with the annual boosters. When we finally did
the Treatment, I was old and tired. I probably would've
died in a decade or two.

"You probably know most of the hype about how
we were the pioneers of the longevity revolution, but
it was much more than that. Yes, the age reversal was
everything we'd imagined," he said, "and there were
side effects no one had imagined. All my life I'd been
heterosexual. Almost immediately after the Treatment,
however, I found myself attracted to women as well as
men."

"But we have heterosexual partners now," I said,
thinking of my own male partner. I was puzzled.

"I mean exclusively, Andrea. Our relationships were
generally with only one person of the opposite sex at
a time. Now I can barely remember when same-sex
mating was considered odd. Or what it was like to be
attracted to just one gender."

I'd heard of heterosexual societies, but what must
it have been like to actually live in one? I thought about
how my life had been like before my partners and I
joined. Now it took all three of us to just keep the family
running, and we were hoping to soon find a fourth. I
couldn't imagine just being with one person.

"You're saying that the First Treatment was
responsible for changing the entire social structure?"
That certainly wasn't in the histories.

He nodded.

"For almost a century, without even realizing it,
my sexuality had set limits on the way I related to the
world. Becoming free from that part of my old self after
the First Treatment gave me more of life to explore. All
twelve of us took full advantage of this new freedom,
and, as we opened more Treatment centers, it wasn't
long before others adopted our lifestyle."

I felt something next to me and turned around. My

arm almost bumped into the shiny, steel tube of the doc-tech, which had silently approached from behind.

"Jorge92A2020?" it asked, its sensors blinking red and green as it moved past me.

"Yes," Jorge replied.

Slender black and silver automated hoses snaked around him, first to scrape skin cells for a DNA identity samples and suction his forearm to check vital signs, followed by a swishing sound as the first prep drugs were injected. It glided back across the room.

"Before we go on, let me check my facts—you were one of eight from the original group who took the Second Treatment?" I was getting more anxious with only ten minutes left before Jorge's Fourth Treatment began.

"Yes, one decided she'd already lived long enough," he said, "and three of the others had died in accidents of one sort or another."

"Then two of you became male following that Treatment?"

"Almost immediately I realized my body chemistry was changing radically," he said. "Within a year, my female breasts atrophied to nubs. Within five years of the Second Treatment, I'd grown a penis and become a fully functioning male."

"What caused your gender switch?"

"After years of testing, they still don't have all the answers. It occurs about twenty percent of the time following the Second Treatment."

"What was the change like?"

"As I said, start by thinking of what your growing bones felt like. This was worse, because I was older."

"Then you were male for a century?"

"A feminist, turned male." He shook his head. "I was a mother for the first time at age fifty, and a father at two-fifty. By that time, we had learned that longevity treatments don't work as well on men, so I wasn't complaining about the change," he said. I laughed like I understood the joke.

"We had no way to know until then that 'born' males wouldn't rejuvenate as well as 'born' females," he explained.

"Eventually, that meant too many females."

Doors hissed behind me and a gurney bearing a sleeping woman in a yellow wrap floated down the corridor along the sensor track outside our glass-walled room toward the bright yellow doors of the adjoining Life Treatment room.

"Why isn't any of your family here today?"

He sat motionless for a moment, then sighed.

"Since the Third Treatment, I've become something of an embarrassment. A freak. One of the things about living a long time is that as you reveal different expressions of yourself, you discover how alone you are," he said. "You can also discover how much you're part of everything."

The doc-tech interrupted, wrapping a hose around Jorge's arm to pump in more drugs. I checked the time again. Five minutes until he would be leaving.

"Okay," I said, when the doc-tech left, "back to the Third Treatment. I saw that five of the original twelve made it to the three-hundred-year mark."

"Yes, but only three of us took the Treatment that did this," he pointed to his face. "By that time, the rest had either died or decided to live the rest of their life unchanged. Within days after the Third Treatment, we had excruciating headaches that lasted weeks at a time. I would've done anything to stop the pain. We required constant monitoring and they even strapped us to our beds, otherwise none of us would've survived."

I watched his ancient face closely, caught up in the transformation as he relived it.

"The doctors' measurements soon confirmed what the mirror already showed us," he said. "Our brains reconfigured to the new shapes of our skulls—the front lobes shrinking and the rear portions growing. Our body hair also grew coarser and longer, and covered more of our bodies. The whole skeletal system was affected.

Within three tortuous years, all our teeth were pushed out by these things." He bared his yellowed incisors.

"You became Neo-Neanderthals."

"An unfortunate nickname," he said. "People obviously saw the physical resemblance, but for some it seemed more ominous than just appearances because of a prank. An intern at the Treatment Center took one of the handhelds and convinced a nearby museum's administrator to allow him to scan a Neanderthal skull. He superimposed it on a scan of my skull from the medical files. We could've been brothers."

"How did you deal with that comparison?"

"It wasn't always easy. So many people equate the past with devolution." He looked me in the eyes, challenging me to deny it.

I looked down and fiddled with the scanner controls. I didn't know where he was going with this.

"You know, whether humans and Neanderthals had a common ancestor is not the issue. My physical appearance doesn't prove it either way if you accept that only minute genetic differences separate all the species on the planet. Besides, the research is inconsistent. Every decade or so, research proves conclusively that Homo sapiens are descendants of Neanderthals, only to be reversed by other evidence. It's been an ongoing controversy for as long as I've been alive."

"What happened to the others who took the Third Treatment?"

"Supposedly accidents," he said, examining the wiry hair on the backs of his thick-skinned hands. "When they found out what we'd become, they didn't survive the decades it took to recover from the shock and anger."

"How was it for you?"

"I think the hardest part was looking at the others and knowing that's what I looked like to them. It was nothing like the reality of who I was. It wasn't until after the others died that I decided I'd have to do something differently to survive. Nothing in my three hundred years of experience had prepared me for being so different, so alienated. I felt there had to be something I was uniquely suited to do to make sense of why I was the way I was. I began to realize that with each of my transformations, I'd become less of who I was when I was born, but more of what my genes remember of who I am as a human."

"You mean you see yourself as more human now than before?" I asked, checking his primitive features to see if he was joking again, but he wasn't smiling.

"You think being human is all in the body?" Jorge asked.

"Where else could it be?" I asked.

"The mind," he said. "The soul. Humanity is more than physical attributes."

"What do you think will happen to you now?"

"Who can say? Maybe I'll become telepathic. Or asexual," he said, with a wink I found disconcerting. "Maybe I'll become who I always was."

"Jorge, why are you going ahead with this? After what you went through, now no one ever goes beyond the Second Treatment." The doc-tech returned, this time ready to escort Jorge 92A2020 to his Fourth Treatment.

"Wait," he told it. "You'll have to be curious enough to find the answer," Jorge said, as he reached over with a thick-skinned hand to gently pat me on the shoulder. I guess he could hear the panic in my voice. "After all, it's nothing more than puberty, and you remember what that's like." As he stood, he reached inside his wrap and handed me an image cube. "I know you were having some problems with your research. I hope these help."

My media scanner whirred and followed Jorge's stooped form as he crossed the room, recording the muffled sounds his cloth slippers made on the granite floor. The final shot was a zoom-in on the gnarled trunk of the Renu Tree of Life as the Advanced Treatment room doors hissed shut behind him. I remained sitting in the booth, examining the four rare images on the cube he handed me. One showed the Neo-Neanderthal Jorge was today, another was him as a round-faced man. The oldest image was of him as a smiling young girl on her bicycle. The fourth image was a close-up of Jorge sometime before his Second Treatment—a slender Eurasian woman with almond-shaped brown eyes and long, strawberry blonde hair. She looked a lot like me.

I could almost feel my growing bones aching.

For more, visit: twfendley.com

Bata Scoir

Kathy L. Brown

Master Enoch spent a disheartening hour beating children after lessons ended then walked the two miles to the cliffs. He trusted the fine weather would distract him from the discouraging turn of events in his classroom that day.

In 1850 Ireland was a beggar of a country lying on Great Britain's doorstep, and Master Enoch had come to save it. A progressive man of noble intentions, he aimed to break the cycle—poverty, disloyalty, crime—through the children and so obtained a teaching post in the fishing village of Portballintae.

Because a command of proper English was the children's only hope for success in British society, he forbade the Irish language in his classroom. Tally sticks, notched each time they spoke the grunting vernacular, ensured fair punishment. At first, they lapsed into Irish often, and he was forced to beat them accordingly. They'd sulked all winter, speaking neither Irish nor English.

But Master Enoch believed, through the power of language, he could unfetter them from their race's twin burdens of superstition and sloth and release their natural human aspirations toward progress. And at last success was at hand; each morning the entire class greeted him with "Good morrow, Master Enoch," and one of the brighter boys could recite the entire

Lord's Prayer in passable English. The schoolmaster had felt hopeful until today—this first spring day.

A strange new girl slid into the classroom almost unnoticed, a thin, barefoot child with cold, blue skin.

"Sit up front, then," he directed her.

The students crossed themselves, muttering popish superstitions, and gave her wide berth on the bench.

"Your name?"

"Is misé Silé." Her voice was cold and gray.

He held up a tally stick. "You know what this is?"

She peered up at him through the matted black hair that hung across her face. "Bata scoir."

"No. 'Tally stick.' We speak English here, Sheila."

But she spoke Irish all day, and the rest soon joined her. The day felt endless, hours suspended between each swing of the wall clock's brass pendulum, as they snickered behind his back. At last the clock struck three, the time of dismissal.

"Sheila, fetch me my hickory switch, near to the door." Their tally sticks full of marks, the students lined up, dumb as beasts, for their punishment. Sheila appeared at the head of the queue and gave over the switch.

Even as he suffocated in her cold gray eyes, he whipped her bare legs. "This hurts me—" he said, "—more than you. Remember respect. Obedience."

Master Enoch was too agitated to sit quietly at his landlady's for tea, so he took his favorite walk to clear his mind. Lost in recollection as he rambled, he ignored the tricks of light and shadow among the land's new greenery.

Ignored the warm meadow's murmur.

Ignored the random cold chills on what was actually quite a hot afternoon.

He clamored among the red basalt columns of the Giant's Causeway, happy to struggle against an adversary that he could overcome by mere hard work. From the highest point he could see Scotland across the channel. Just a glimpse lifted his spirits, for he'd never been so discouraged.

But the weather in Ulster can turn in a twinkle. In the few moments he spent tossing breadcrumbs for the petrels to snatch in midair, mist off the sea wrapped about him, and the sky grew gray. Blindfolded by fog, he hesitated. He could hear the waves breaking across the Causeway below and tried to remember which way lead to safety. The fog nuzzled even closer; its dark, cold breath soaked through his clothes. He rubbed his eyes with invisible, black-gloved hands. It was no good; he could see nothing.

Then, a noise in the distance—wood striking wood. Tap. Tap. Tap.

"Ha-llo," he shouted. "Call out. I can't see my way."

The tapping grew louder. The source: to the right. No, the left, it seemed. But who would spend teatime out here in the rain and the fog? Other than a melancholy schoolmaster who hadn't noticed gray clouds trooping in from the west, blotting out the fresh blue and white of a fine spring afternoon? "Direct me, I beg you. I'm likely to fall off the cliff."

Only tapping in reply. Did the tapping of sticks have local significance? Perhaps it was a common signal in this land of sudden mists and easy misstep. But the sound echoed in the fog; he could make no sense of its source's direction.

A dismal thought sent him to near panic: suppose it wasn't a man? What if he were shouting for help from a foraging beast or insect-hunting bird? His lungs full of wet fog, he struggled to bleat, "Please! Please speak."

The rhythmic tapping was now very close. Surely some person was there, some kind soul who intended to help. Perhaps the landlady had sent her simpleton nephew to fetch him back. His boots soaked through to his stockings, he shivered. "Though you will not—cannot, speak, I trust you mean me well."

Reaching out, he stepped toward

the sound. And then stumbled, clutching at wisps of salt air.

END

A special acknowledgement to Matt Morrison (Matha Ó Muiresasáin), who shared his grandparents' childhood recollections of the tally sticks at an Irish language (Gaeilge) class I attended.

For more, visit: kathylbrown.com

THE THINGS I LEFT BEHIND

Uma Eachempati

On my annual visit to India, I asked Mother where she had kept a cardboard box containing some of my papers, since she had relocated in my absence. Pointing to a room filled with boxes stacked up to the ceiling, she said "It is there." On my next visit when I enquired about the box she showed me the storage room with a few boxes in a corner saying, "It is there." I looked through them but could not find MY box.

I had left India for the USA with a pair of children aged seven and three. Two boxes each were what the airlines allowed. We left our motherland, our families and stable jobs to seek our fortune in the West, leaving the familiar behind; to see the world and the traditional "broadening the horizon."

Furniture, kitchen appliances, books and clothes were sold or distributed appropriately. But a medium-sized cardboard box was left in Mother's safekeeping. The box contained mementos including diaries written during the pre-teen years. They could not have been very interesting, as page after page would have been, "Who does she (my mother) think she is?" She did not allow my sister or me to visit friends or go to the movies with them. We could only accompany our parents or grandmother for any outings. She laid down the rules and smelt trouble a mile away. Our friends would visit us but we were not to go to their houses

- they had BROTHERS. She kept us away from boys as much as possible so that we "did not get into trouble."

In spite of mother's watchful eye, I received letters during the summer holidays from a boy of my class who obtained my address from the boy next door. They hung out on the street in front of the house knowing that I was at my desk near the window upstairs, somewhat like the balcony scene of Romeo and Juliet. The scene was mundane and silent, with undercurrents of thrill and romance. The coy glances and the appealing replies went back and forth. Mother noticed and closed the lower shutters of the window, without any explanation most of the time, with an occasional "There is too much glare."

The following year I was home again.

"Ma! You remember my cardboard box full of my papers, do you know where it could be?"

Mother was silent for a while. "You know that Subbamma who was working for us for a few years, she was selling things from the house. Some of my little bronze sculptures as well as the fancy embroidered tablecloths and napkins are also missing. I don't know, maybe she sold your papers too."

"But what could she do with my letters and my diary. Who would want them?"

I did not want to tell her the contents of my box. It was a secret from my mother even though I was not an adolescent any longer but a grown woman with two children.

"She must have sold it as scrap paper. Any small amount was good enough for her," Mother said.

"Why did she want anything? She had her own room and three meals a day and you would give her sarees for major festivals. She had no relatives in town to give presents to ..."

"She needed money to buy beedis, she smoked all the time. Being diabetic, had a craving for sweets. She bribed the young boy down the street to run her errands."

I was dejected. Mother sounded matter of fact and oblivious to my broken heart. She didn't understand.

"You know the time when I was away for a month to take care of Grandma," Mother interrupted my thoughts, "Subbamma had the run of the house. She died soon after in a diabetic coma. I did not have the chance to question her. Gradually, I realized the many small items that were missing. She would not take anything obvious like the TV."

Mother stumbled to explain while mourning the loss of her own mother. Was my loss greater than hers? I tried to console myself but still counted my losses.

"Ma, I think my autograph book was also there. You know the little book with a red cover."

"Did you have Gandhi's autograph in there?"

"Yes, I did."

Mahatma Gandhi had come to town for a political rally in the forties. Obtaining special permission for a five-minute interview, Grandma, Mother, my sister and me pushed through crowds to enter a room, where Gandhi was seated cross-legged on a cot leaning against a bolster. Timidly my sister and me extended our autograph books. He signed in Hindi and English. Mother paid five rupees for each signature to his secretary, the money going towards the Harijan fund for the uplift of the untouchables,

"It also had Alexander Fleming," I said sadly. Dr Fleming was on a trip to Madras and there was a lecture by him on his discovery of the antibiotic, Penicillin. This was in the fifties. I was pleased to have seen a great scientist. Autograph collecting was a good way to be near celebrities.

"And Ma!" I said after a lull in the conversation. "It also had that upcoming political figure. Do you remember? He said, 'Children, where are your autograph books, bring them I will sign them for you and so he did in three languages- Hindi, English and Telugu, across two pages."

"He never made it anywhere," Mother smiled." He had great hopes about himself," she added.

Every other moment I remembered yet another of the contents of the box. It had my school magazine where two of my short stories were published, stories of love and murder as viewed by a fourteen-year-old.

"Irreplaceable, Ma, how could you be so careless?" I moaned in silence.

Next morning sounds of activity awoke me. Cow bells jingling, dogs barking, children running and anxious men clanging bells of their bicycles, asking pedestrians to move out of their path. Morning progressed and people filled the streets.

The vegetable vendor knocked on the door to enquire if we needed any fresh vegetables for the day. We were regular customers. Another vendor sauntered down the street once a week shouting "Vessels for old clothes!" We collected old clothes for him. He appraised them for their worth in steel ware. Shirts, pants and silk sarees being in great demand. Sarees torn or faded that he discarded were used to mop floors or polish furniture and brassware. Those in good condition were given to the domestics but Mother had to be diplomatic. The staff would imagine favoritism and mumble behind her back. At Diwali - the festival of lights - they were given new clothes in appreciation of their hard work and loyalty. Other vendors bought old bottles and tins, selling them to a dealer. We were paid to be rid of our junk. All these transactions took place on our front verandah.

The paper man bought paper of every shape and size. Newspapers assessed higher than school notebooks. Street urchins rummaged the streets for paper, big or small, every valuable piece collected in big bags. Vendors who set up small stalls along the sidewalk used the smaller pieces. They twirled a sheet into a cone and filled it up with fried peanuts or other snacks. Larger pieces of paper were used to parcel at the grocery store. We wrapped school text books with the colorful ones. Paper was a precious commodity. It was also sacred, representing the Goddess of learning. It was to be respected and not stepped on.

I brooded about my precious box. One of the boys in college had given me a silver bracelet with two silver hearts with our names inscribed, dangling from the chain. Over three summers he proclaimed his love. These mementos of my teen years, I did not bring to the USA.

I lay in bed pondering my past, placing those moments in a life line. What significance would this moment be on my deathbed? Memories of parents, children, husband, friends. Would I be thinking of this bracelet and the boy who gave it to me? He wore thick glasses and a thick moustache. I looked away every time his eyes pierced into mine. I was at the beach accompanied by adults and he was there hanging around, swallowing me from a distance. Beaming glimpses across sea breeze and sand. It was a strong and deep grown up feeling. At the time it did not seem childish.

My agony spilled over into imagination. Maybe a young couple walking along the Marina decided to buy fried peanuts. Looking at the wrapping paper, the jubilant boy on his first outing saw terms of endearment and proclamations of love in well formed, round shaped words written in blue ink. Did the boy give it to his sweetheart as if written by him? "My dearest love. I have been dreaming of you in my arms, absorbed in your brown eyes and touching your soft cheeks all night. The little dimple that lights up your face when you smile…."

Or did the two read it together and have a laugh and wonder where the writer and the recipient of the letter were. Did they get married and live forever in bliss? They had heard of a message in a bottle but not a message in a packet of peanuts. I chuckled, blowing away my disappointment of not being able to preserve the thrills of my teen years.

"Ma," I said giving her a hug. "Can love letters be recycled?"

Edna's Attic

Gerald Dlubala

Edna sat as usual, in her wine-colored velour rocker/recliner next to an end table filled with crumpled Kleenex, a couple of pens that likely wouldn't work even with a good lick or heat put to them, a coaster from her now passed parents' trip to Las Vegas some thirty years ago, and an ashtray that regularly reminds her of the nasty habit that she at times, still craves. The well-worn chair provides an outline and indentations of her aging body in an almost ghostly form when she gets up, but that's not often anymore. She's gotten pretty comfortable sleeping in the chair, usually nodding off just before the late news. Her real bed doesn't appeal to her ever since her husband... disappeared.

That's what they'll tell you anyway.

She repeats that to herself often, but in her heart, she knows different. She knows what happened to him, but no one believed her then, and they certainly wouldn't believe her now. Distraught was the term they used to describe her. Terms like "an emotional wreck, senile," and even just "plain crazy" became commonplace in their whispers, almost exclusively behind her back. She heard them all, even if they thought they were being discreet.

But now, well, that damn little Styrofoam ball, the kind we used to pop on our car antennas to look cool, she would always think, just keeps bouncing down the steps that lead to their attic, now her attic, and dammit, she's just tired of it. And all that other ruckus that continues to go on up there too.

Let's face it though, she's tired in general, mostly just existing rather than living. And being called out as a looney bird whenever she decides to go out in public doesn't help. She's looked on as the town crazy lady, and boy wasn't that an eye-opener, she would say to herself when she found out through the gossip grapevine.

There's a new crazy lady in town and it's ME!

But she couldn't help it if no one wanted to believe the truth. The truth that she witnessed with her own damn eyes, by the way.

But I'm the crazy one, she frequently repeated to herself, at least daily.

Nevertheless, she hadn't made the trek up those attic stairs for nearly three years, and just barely before then. Miles, her late husband, would go up there only when needed to clean attic vents, chase out any critters that tried to make a squatter's home up there, or even to check on wiring and such. He didn't like it though.

"There's bad juju up there Edna," he would say. "It's like something's up there in the shadows watching me, focused on me. I can damn near feel it, Edna. I can feel it. Bad juju."

He'd do whatever he had to do and then get the hell out of there and scurry back downstairs. It got to the point that he would sometimes come down in such a rush that he would leave his tools and anything else he took with him up there and then have to buy more tools for the house downstairs. He sure wouldn't go back up there to just get tools. That wasn't a good enough reason, no sir.

Then the big storm came. Thunder, lightning, and rain like nobody had ever witnessed in these parts before. And the wind. Lordy, that wind sure sounded like a tornado, but the local weather guy said it was just wind and that's all.

Would he even know the difference? He seemed so young and inexperienced.

Either way, Miles had to venture up in that attic to secure a vent cover that came loose in the wind, banging furiously against the house. It couldn't have been any louder if somebody was out there with a 20-pound sledgehammer banging away on the side of the house. He was hesitant for sure, but he'd always try to put up a strong front for Edna.

He procrastinated for a while, and then when the banging got even louder, he took a deep breath, exhaled, grasped the red ball that he recently reattached to the end of the rope connected to the attic door in the ceiling, and slowly pulled the stairway down to the landing, You didn't have to look up to notice the flashes of lightning reaching in through the vent openings and windows, disrupting the pitch-black backdrop and painting all sorts of eerie moving shadows. The noise increased in intensity with the opening of the attic door, leaving Miles no choice but to go up there and see what was going on. Behind him, out of his direct sight, Edna instinctively crossed herself as if she was in church.

"Be careful Miles."

"Yep, be back down as soon as I can."

That was the last time Edna saw her husband of twenty-five years. As he got to the second-highest step, where he usually was able to reach and pull the string to turn on the hanging bulb light, some mighty ferocious and angry sounds erupted, drowning out the worst thunder, winds, and rain that the town had seen. *It was the sound of hell*, Edna would later tell the police. In a matter of seconds, she swore that she saw both of his feet lifted off of the ladder and the attic door immediately slamming shut. Then, complete silence.

It was...was like the attic ate him.

Before she could even realize what happened, feverishly pulling on the red ball to open the attic back up, the storm blew over, the skies cleared, and the noise of the loose banging vent had stopped. When the investigation took place, no loose vents, shutters or anything else around the house was found or noted. All tight and secure, and nothing up in the attic to be afraid of.

"Yes, we're sure of that," said Officer Townsend.

Edna was broken, not knowing where to turn or what to think. Officer Townsend volunteered to stay with her as long as needed, not only to offer support but to talk to her and try and figure out just what happened. What *really* happened.

Was there ever a "Miles" here to begin with?

"For now, Edna," said Officer Townsend, "With no real clues as to what happened, all we can do is file a missing person report."

Neither Miles, or any remnant of him, was ever found, and as Edna told her story to anyone that would listen, she acquired the label of being a little flaky, making up this story for attention and maybe a little pity. When she started to withdraw from the townsfolk and turn almost hermit-like, her persona grew to be simply, the crazy lady.

"Her husband probably just left," they would say behind Edna's back. "Found his chance to get away from the crazy lady and took it. Likely had that vent loose on purpose so he could get out and go missing" they said.

But Edna never doubted what she saw, so she became a recluse, complete with a duct-taped attic door that was never going to be opened again. Never. No matter what. Even though the noises continued. Not every night, but most of them.

She just mostly kept to herself since no one would listen to or believe her anymore anyway, not the crazy lady. And she didn't have the resources to leave, so she'd just gotten used to turning the television up louder and falling asleep in her rocker recliner, going out for necessities at odd times of the day or night when needed, rarely talking to anyone and barely making eye contact.

Some life, huh? she would ask herself. And then just as quickly give herself a scolding for talking to herself.

Jeez, maybe you are crazy.

But the ball. That damn red ball that was tied on the attic rope for so long and sucked up on that stormy night just won't go away. Damn near every night, Edna witnessed that little red ball bouncing down the steps as if someone cracked that attic door open and cut it loose to bounce down the stairs and land on the fourth step. Always the fourth step, right at the landing of the stairway where it turns to go towards the attic.

This is nuts. My mind is playing tricks. But every night? Oh Edna, maybe you are the new crazy lady.

Sometimes those thoughts brought a little smile to her face, but they wore on her just the same. She tried to focus on other things, but the attic was getting to her, working on her mental condition, wearing her down and stressing her out. Some nights she swore she could even hear Miles calling her from up there, in need of help. She sometimes thought about going up there, but then her common sense prevailed, reminding her that the attic was fully inspected and checked out the night she reported her husband's...misfortune.

Then, one night while Edna dozed on her favorite chair, she was startled and jumped as if slapped in the face at the sound of something in the attic being slid across the floor. Her eyes tracked a path across the ceiling following the sound she heard. Or thought she heard. Her heart raced. She instinctively brought her hand up to her chest. Her heartbeat thumped against her opened palm. Shaking, she reached for the phone sitting on the end table.

Should I call the sheriff? What do I say, that the ghosts are particularly noisy tonight? They'll take me away for sure.

Edna decided against the phone call and remained in her chair, looking upward and listening. No more noises, no more scratching or scuffling. Silence. It was almost scarier than the noises because it seemed to be a complete and total silence. Absolutely everything was quiet, even her old refrigerator that always made some sort of buzzing or whirring noise.

Edna popped the footrest of her favorite velour rocker/recliner down with a backward donkey kick, stood up, pulled down and straightened her sweater, and walked to the stairway leading to the attic. The red ball was sitting on the stair tread of the fourth step, right at the landing of the stairway, as usual. She took a long blink, hoping that upon opening her eyes, that red ball would be back on the rope hanging from the attic door and that she just imagined it on the step. She would be wrong, of course.

She confidently picked the red ball up. Holding the rope with one hand and the red Styrofoam ball in the other, she brought them together just as she had done hundreds of times before. As she strung the rope through the hole in the ball, she started hearing the rumblings from above. The door to the attic quivered and shook, almost as if someone was up there stomping up and down on the door, warning her to stay away. She tied a knot in the rope after threading it through the ball, watched it dangle there in front of her, dancing and bobbing with the vibrations of the attic door. In one bold and powerful move, Edna first pulled the duct tape off of the seams of the attic door, then pulled the door down using both hands. She jerked hard enough that the door slammed down, partially pulling the screws out of the ladder supports on one side. For a moment her concentration broke.

Now, who is gonna fix that crap?

She tested the first step of the ladder to make sure she didn't damage that as well, then looked up into the darkness. The loud darkness. Thoughts ran through her mind, with images of ratty old dolls with crazed eyes, sinister clowns drooling through their tattered, sharp fangs, or giant spiders with webs strong enough to trap anyone or anything that it came in contact with.

But what she saw wasn't anything like that at all. There was simply darkness.

Almost too dark, she thought. *A dark not of this world.*

No, she didn't see anything scary at all. But she felt it. It was a feeling that bolted through her body from her eyes down through her legs, which she noticed were beginning to feel a little rubbery.

Juju. Bad juju. This is what he meant!

She changed her mind about going up there and stepped down from the first step of the ladder, but her hands were stuck to the attic ladder rails, attached as if they were part of the ladder itself. The ladder started to raise back up with her desperately trying to release herself. The noise became deafening. Like the worst storm these parts ever experienced. Like the sounds of hell. Her screams were silent.

Who would hear me anyway?

Her feet were lifted off the floor. A blinding flash of lightning followed by the unmistakable roar of rolling thunder. She was sucked up to the attic, still attached to the ladder. The door slammed shut as tight as the day it was installed. Ceiling fixtures rattled. The red Styrofoam ball dangled from the attic rope. It swayed back and forth for a few seconds, became silent, and hung straight and true. Then it fell, bouncing down to the fourth step, right at the landing that leads to the attic door.

Bad juju.

Eighteen months later the For Sale sign still stood in the yard in front of Miles and Edna's house. Inside was Pam Josten, a recently licensed realtor showing the house to Ben and Julie Hoskins, newlyweds looking for their first starter home.

"As you can see, it's a bit of a fixer-upper," said Pam. "Been abandoned for over a year now. The woman that lived here became a kind of recluse after her husband left, and then eventually decided to abandon the property. The bank took it over and has been providing the necessary maintenance outside to keep it from being an eyesore, but it would obviously benefit from a little TLC. It looks like a lot of work, but a lot of it is just aesthetics, surface work, and easy fixes if you're handy. And I'm thinking you could get it for a really good price."

"Yeah, it needs some work," said Ben. "Even a good cleaning and fresh paint would go a long way. And a couple of those upstairs vents and shutters look a little loose and crooked. We'll have to make sure there's no birds or anything living up there. And what's that? Looks like a little ball or something on the steps."

"Oh, looks like the pull for the attic door," said Pam. "Must've come off the rope from the access door right there."

Pam picked up the red Styrofoam ball from the fourth step and quickly threaded it onto the attic pull rope and tied it off.

"See," said Pam. "Another easy fix. Already one less thing to do"

Julie looked at Ben and smiled. All three walked towards the front door in agreement that at the right price, this could be the starter home that Ben and Julie were looking for.

As they were closing the front door, no one noticed the red ball bouncing down the stairs, settling on the fourth step, right at the landing, where the stairway turns toward the attic door.

For more, visit: gldlubala.com

FOUR'S A CROWD

Kevin P. Sheridan

Maggie Moo stood at attention on the living room couch with the oversized cushions, anticipation and longing evident on her face. The living room was large and carpeted with vaulted ceilings and a large picture window overlooking the woods. It was perfect for watching the day pass outside. Her tail was wagging slowly like a metronome setting perfect time for the music only she could hear. According to her Master, Maggie Moo *was simply the most adorable two-year-old Chorkie pup*. Of course, the Master was the authority on such matters, so it must be true.

Maggie Moo's half-brother, Charlie, stared up at her and Callie the Calico with his ears up and his white-tipped tail also wagging in time with some unheard music. His eyes - one blue and one brown - were wide with excitement, shifting from Maggie Moo to Callie and back again to Maggie Moo. Callie, the resident cat, lazed on the back of the couch merely staring at Charlie through half-closed eyes, a quiet purr rolled up her body and through her throat.

"Is it time yet?" came a barking shout from Charlie.

Every muscle fiber in Charlie's small but thick chest was twitching to run. This place was not his home, but his surroundings were not unfamiliar as he had spent a lot of time visiting Callie, Maggie Moo and Louie. Louie, a Sugar Bear, didn't get out of the wire-mesh cage he called home often, but he was still very much a part of the clan. Charlie's focus stayed on Maggie Moo and Callie. He whined with a combination of excitement and anticipation, tapping his paws on the floor in short bursts of energy – up-down – pause – up-down, up-down – pause – up-down.

When the commotion began, Louie was lying in his heated pouch contemplating a nap. Daylight was his time to sleep and reenergize for play time during the night. His cage was darkened on all sides by a heavy, blue blanket and only the front provided a nearly full view of the room. Peeking out of his pouch, he could see the offending party making the shrill whining noise that roused him from his near slumber. He had a feeling that his nap was over.

"Come on. Come on. Come on! Isn't it time to go yet?" asked Charlie looking at Maggie Moo, then Callie, and back to Maggie Moo again.

"Hold on to your tail a moment," Maggie Moo said. "It's not time yet. Just wait. Be patient."

"Yeah, right!" said Callie. "That's like asking a ball not to roll downhill and you know what that will do to him."

"Ball? Where?" said Charlie looking around excitedly and hopping in small circles while he did so.

"Would y'all be quiet. I am trying to take a nap here," said Louie in a gruff and chuffing voice. The chuffing coming from Louie's throat sounded like a small engine turning over and coughing but never quite catching. He was hanging upside down from the front wall of his cage making his furry, white belly visible to the others.

Maggie Moo knew what was about to happen. She could barely stifle her own whimper at the thought of her Master saying the word park. She knew what that word meant – wide open spaces to run and an array of so many smells that she couldn't possibly sniff them all. The trick would be to make it through the living room, kitchen, and into her Master's truck while fighting off

Charlie's excitement and haphazard, uncontrollable weaving back and forth to do the same. Charlie wasn't much heavier than Maggie Moo, but he was taller and faster. The last time they darted for the truck, they bumped and twisted on and over each other the whole way. She had to resort to growling and nipping at Charlie to get him out of her way.

"Hey Mags," Callie inquired in a teasing tone while licking her paw and wiping her face. "Are you going to let that pooch run over you again?"

"He didn't run me over! I'll have you know I had it all under control."

"Yes, he did," said Louie, a laughing chuff, chuff, chuff coming from his throat (*the engine almost starting that time*). "He nearly ran straight through you! As I recall, you were left sniffing his butt."

"What do you know about it?" Maggie Moo asked, now sitting down on the couch.

"Yeah *Inmate*!" Callie chimed in. "What of it?"

Chuff.

"Let's play," said Charlie looking at Maggie Moo and Callie eagerly and having retrieved a small, yellow ball that was now sitting between his legs.

Callie stopped her grooming and looked around the living room. She could see an assortment of toys from a small, wicker toy box spread across the entire floor of the room. These were Maggie Moo's toys, but Charlie had been playing with them. Maggie Moo didn't usually like Charlie playing with her toys. Callie continued slowly looking around the room but showed no desire to move her large frame and thick coat of fur, let alone play with this overly eager short-haired mutt with a case of the jitters.

"No thanks, *Ball Boy*," said Callie continuing to groom her face.

"Ball boy? That's not my name."

"If you're so eager to play, and the word *fetch* is the name of the game for a dog, then Ball Boy will suit you just fine."

"Hey! Just because you are fat

and lazy doesn't mean you can't come down here and play with me. Come on, try it. It'll be fun!"

"Oh, wait…let me restate that, I don't *want* to play with you."

"Give it up, Charlie," Maggie Moo said. "She never plays with anyone unless she is moving from one lounging spot to another and then its only to smack you if you get in her way."

"Aw," Charlie drawled out the word into a howl. "There's nothing in this room to do. My Master is gone and locked me in here with you guys. Come on, when are we going to go?"

"Better in here, Ball Boy, than the rodent's cage," Callie said looking around the room at Louie. "The convict over there rules his prison yard, but you'd have a hard time fitting in there. Besides, it looks like you've got plenty to play with already." Callie returned her gaze to Charlie for a moment, and then lifted her nose to the air and turned her head slightly away from Charlie as if giving him the cold shoulder.

Louie quietly chuffed and said, "Who are you calling a convict?" Chuff, chuff (*the engine sputtered and died*).

Besides, Louie thought worriedly, *there is absolutely no way Charlie would fit into my cage – my yard – my home!* Chuff, chuff, chuff (*the engine began overheating now*). *What was Callie thinking?* Chuff. *Did she really think Charlie could possibly be put into his home?* Chuff! Chuff! *Could that happen?*

"I hope my Master hurries," Charlie said. "The last time it took this long I peed on my blanket and my Master had to wash it. I could tell by the tone of voice my Master was not very happy with me. I really gotta play." He stood wagging his tail faster than before as if it were on some speed dial being turned up to high. Charlie lowered his head and front half of his body and said, "Come on! Let's play! You could help me take my mind off of the peeing thing. We'd have so much fun."

Callie shifted slightly. Her grooming done, she

tucked her paws under her girth. Her eyes were slits as if sleep was about to consume her. She slowly turned her head away from Charlie.

"PLAY!"

The high-pitched bark caused Callie's ears to lay back and her paws to come out from under her chest. Her eyes went wide as she stared and leaned away from Charlie.

"PLAY! PLAY! PLAY!"

Charlie hopped up onto the couch, now only inches away from Callie. Louie ran around his cage once and stopped at the back of his cage, hidden by the shadow, and stared out at the spectacle before him. He wondered if Charlie realized he was about to get a beating!

"Don't do it, Ball Boy," Louie advised.

"PLAY!"

Callie's ears continued to lay back in annoyance. Her eyes stared at him like daggers aimed to kill. She forced air from her lungs through her throat and out of her mouth, making a guttural, static white-noise sound – spitting while she did. Charlie's white flag wagged even faster in pure excitement.

Louie looked on in anticipation as he could see ahead of time what was about to unfold. "Oh, that stupid mutt doesn't have a clue!" Louie said. "Mag's, can't you do something with that?"

"With what?" Maggie Moo asked. "Oh, Charlie? As long as he isn't playing with my toys, I don't care."

Charlie sneezed and shook his head once and looked at Callie with wide eyes, barking and whining and preparing to jump. His tail was wagging so fast now that it was nearly invisible.

"I will make you play with me."

"Cut it out, Charlie. You are playing with fire," Maggie Moo said. She had come to her attention stance once again on the couch and looked at Charlie and Callie.

"No, you won't, Ball Boy," Callie hissed.

As Charlie prepared to let out another high-pitched bark, Callie's right front paw lashed out with blinding speed. Three swats of her paw, the first striking Charlie's head and the following two his snout, could be heard in rapid successions. Whack, whack, whack! Charlie could not pull away in time to avoid the strikes, and Callie was back in her original position before he could even flinch.

"Hey!" Charlie said shaking his head, sneezing, and sitting down all at the same time. "What gives? I was only trying to play with you."

From his darkened cage, Louie chuffed again, but this time it was with a snicker of satisfaction at the yelp from the mutt. *Smack down*, he thought, *and that should end it so I can finally take my nap*. That, however, was wishful thinking on Louie's part.

"I told you, Ball Boy. I am not in the mood. My home, my rules, and you are here as an uninvited guest. This is not the time to play. Besides, four's a crowd."

Charlie used his left paw to massage the side of his snout where Callie had just tagged him. As he rose, a low growl came from deep inside Callie, her tail flicking from side-to-side in snappy arcs, but she gave no indication of either moving away or striking again.

"You better not," Maggie Moo said.

"Hey, Furball! Smack him again!" Chuff, chuff, chuff (*the engine working hard again, trying to come to life*).

His pride wounded and all thoughts of playing now sufficiently snuffed out, Charlie jumped down to the floor, twirled in place three times, and flopped onto the carpet. He rested his chin on his front paws and half turned away from Callie. Louie chuffed several more times. To him, Charlie's resignation looked like pouting.

"Aw!" Louie said in a teasing tone. Chuff. "That figures. Poor Ball Boy can't stand a little rejection. Now can we please have some quiet?" With a sense that the quiet would resume, he retreated back into his pouch to resume his nap.

"Inmate," Charlie growled under his breath.

For a short time, the room fell quiet. Maggie Moo sat back down on the couch but at attention, looking longingly down the hall for some sign her Master was coming. Callie continued lounging on the couch's high cushion, and Charlie lay on the floor pouting. That was where Maggie Moo's Master found them and the coup de grâce came with a racket.

"Do the puppies want to go to the park?" asked the Master to Maggie Moo and Charlie.

That word – oh, that glorious word – *park*. There it was, music to their ears, bringing forth images of green fields, trees, dead leaves, and squirrels. Everything else forgotten, they began to bark, croon, and bounce uncontrollably, patting their paws beneath them as their happy wailings rose to a crescendo. Charlie's bark was shrill and whiny, almost as if he was in pain or hurt by some invisible assailant. Maggie Moo's was also shrill but not as high-pitched as Charlie's. It was what one might expect from a little, Benji-looking dog.

"Yes! Puppies wanna go to the park?" asked the Master in a babyish voice.

There! There it was again! The word *park*. It spawned images, sounds, and smells in their little minds that could no longer be controlled. The room exploded with a flurry of activity and noise. The barks were now met with forward motion. A days' worth of pent up energy burst out of them as they ran for the truck door.

"Oh, my dander!" came Louie's chuffing from the edge of the cage (*this time the engine sounded more like it backfired*). "Please go already!"

"Don't you worry Inmate. They will be gone in a moment," Callie said.

Maggie Moo leapt from the couch and hit the floor in full stride. She sprinted for the hallway that led to the kitchen like a three-year-old thoroughbred making the last turn in the Kentucky Derby. Charlie was up at the same time and came alongside Maggie Moo, bumping her and getting their legs tangled up with each other. The race was on and it was going to be a photo finish.

As Maggie Moo rounded the corner of the hallway, she clipped the corner with her rump, which slowed her pace and sent her sideways crashing into Charlie. Charlie, knocked off balance and thrown to one side, hit the hardwood floor, losing all traction and causing his legs to go out from under him. Regaining his balance, he dug in for purchase and Louie watched and thought it strange that Charlie's legs were moving like a Greyhound at a race, but he wasn't going anywhere as his paws only slid across the slick floor. In an amazing feat of acrobatics and will (*Louie would embellish the story that way later*), Charlie gained traction and caught up to Maggie Moo, who was running for the truck that would take them to the park.

Charlie twirled in circles at the truck door, barking his shrill bark, his white flag madly waving in the air. He leapt into the truck when the door opened and whimpered and shook with excitement. Maggie Moo's legs were too short to allow her to jump into the truck though she wanted to in a most genuine but pitiful way. Maggie Moo was so excited that she started to sing. Her singing was like a drawn-out growl but higher pitched with inflections that matched her excitement. Her Master lifted her up into the cab of the truck with a smile. Maggie Moo and Charlie whined with excitement all the way to the park while hanging their heads out of the truck's window, catching all of the marvelous scents on the air and occasionally spotting a squirrel on the run.

"Can you believe that, Furball?" Louie chuffed (*engine turning over again*) while hanging upside down in his cage. "Are they crazy or what?"

"Crazy as a dog, Inmate. Crazy as a dog," Callie said.

Louie chuffed at this and said, "Time to nap now that I have some peace and quiet. What-chu gonna do?"

But Callie did not answer. Louie could see that she

had already settled in and closed her eyes, opening them sometimes only slightly when she heard an unknown noise. She resumed her purring. Louie hopped down from the wall of his cage, curled up in his pouch that was resting on his heated rock, and began to snooze. The house was pleasantly quiet.

♦ ♦ ♦

When Maggie Moo and Charlie returned, they were significantly less excited. The door to the home opened and they made their way to the water bowl. They lapped up the water until it was nearly gone and when they raised their heads, the water dripped off the fur on their chins. They lounged side-by-side in front of the large window and admired the beautiful day in which they had played. Callie hopped down off of her high perch and sat beside them, carelessly looking out of the window.

"Was it as good for you as it was for me?" Callie asked.

"Wow! What a great time," Charlie said.

"Yes, it was indeed. The park is my most favorite place – except for maybe home," Maggie Moo replied.

"Well, was the park the same as it was the last time you went?" Callie asked.

"Yes, it was," Charlie said.

"Then why make such a fuss over going?"

Charlie thought about it, but it was Maggie Moo who replied. "The park is like nothing else. It's like...dog heaven. You can run free with your fur waving in the air. You can slice through the mown or unmown grass. And the smells! Ha! Don't even get me started on the smells! I'm telling you Callie, it's a dog's heaven."

"Yeah, what she said," Charlie agreed.

"Dog heaven, eh? Well, let me tell you there is nothing like a long afternoon nap to get the blood pumping. Take this afternoon for example. You left, there was peace and quiet, and I slept. Look at me now. I've never felt better! Cat heaven...maybe."

"Ha! Ha!" Charlie said. "As I've said before, that just means you are fat and lazy and getting fatter by the day."

"Touché," Callie said, tipping up her nose to the sky and turning her head away from Charlie.

"No," came a voice from behind them, "Callie's right. There is nothing like an afternoon nap."

This was one of the rare occasions when Louie's Master let him out of his cage. He wandered over to the trio, climbing atop Callie and finding a spot to sit. Callie didn't mind and often allowed Louie this rare pleasure because the rest of his time was spent in the confines of the small cage he called home.

"Hey Inmate. How's it hangin'?" Callie asked, slowly turning her head back.

"Doin' fine, Furball. You?"

"Not bad. Not bad. The noise made it back home."

"I see that," Louie said. "Though much calmer than when they left."

"Why do you call me Ball Boy?" Charlie asked.

They all ignored him.

"We were just discussing our excitement," Maggie Moo said to Louie, "and trying to explain why it means so much to us to go to the park. I guess it's hard to explain because you have never gone outside to play."

"Heck no!" Louie said in an excited tone. "I'd get eaten by some dirty old stinky bird." He shook off a small shiver and said, "I don't even want to think about that – my worst nightmare."

"No one would want to eat you, Inmate," Callie said sarcastically. "You aren't worth the effort for the half a bite they might get."

Charlie looked at Maggie Moo and then at Callie and Louie and said, "Imagine being in the best place, every place all at once, that makes you happy. All at once. Whatever that is for you, imagine being there and how happy that makes you feel. That's what the park is for me."

"Yes, I get that Ball Boy, but do you have to cause such a racket?" Louie asked.

They laughed together and spent the afternoon watching the rest of the day pass by the large window. All four of them were daydreaming about their best day.

The End

For more, visit: kevinpsheridan.com

Phone Booth Ecstasy

Jessica Mathews

James stretched, having just woken up for the day. He rolled off the well-worn leather couch and looked around. Something seemed different about the dorm room-size apartment but James couldn't put his finger on it. He shrugged his shoulders looking at a small clock in the shape of a robin almost faded beyond recognition hanging above the mauve toilet.

"Noon, eh? I wonder what Etna's got to eat around this dump." James struggled to zip his jeans hanging snug around his hips. He didn't wash his hands. Instead, he took five steps from the bathroom to the kitchen, plucking his threadbare I Love New York t-shirt off an ageing Elvis figurine lamp that at one point in the 1970s stopped gyrating its porcelain hips for an unknown reason. James opened the mini-fridge in the apartment kitchenette and quickly closed it again. There were only 2 things James found in the fridge during the half-second look he took before the smell of rotting flesh overwhelmed all of his senses. The two items in the tiny fridge were a putrid package of ground hamburger meat and a jar of pickle juice with one shriveled up pickle still swirling in the moss-colored liquid.

James saw a note from Etna held by a banana-shaped magnet on the mini-fridge door. James ripped the note out from under the cheap magnet. The plastic banana hit the shabby tile with a resounding plink. James didn't notice. Etna kept too much stuff around for him to notice one tiny yellow fake banana plunging to its demise, shattering upon impact with the tile. The note was on paper the color of decay as if Etna had used paper from fifty years ago. He thought nothing of it. Etna was always going through people's houses she cleaned for a living and "liberating" items she either couldn't afford for herself (like extra rolls of toilet paper or toothpaste) or items she though deserved a better home (like hers). Etna probably stole the stationary she wrote her note on from the million-year-old bitty next door. Every time Etna went over there she came home with something or another that smelled like rotting old lady parts and stale perfume from before the Great Depression.

"I'll be on the west side all day working. Meet me at Frankie's at 1 pm."

Frankie's was the nickname of a popular Frankenstein-themed frankfurter cafe by the houses Etna cleaned on Thursdays, which made today Thursday. On Thursdays, James ran pre-bets for weekend events around town. He was always in debt to Simple Simon, his bookie. James knew if he wanted to place bets today he would have to run Simon's errands first.

"Quarters. I need quarters. Where did she hide them this time?" James mumbled to himself as he searched his pockets, Etna's cluttered counter space and her dresser drawers filled with cobwebs and spiders hidden in their nests throughout Etna's underwear. James finally found where Etna hid her money. "Eureka!" In the bathroom James found a mason jar under the sink between the half-used toothpaste tubes and the extra towels, all stolen from different sets from random apartments around the city.

Etna didn't believe in banks. She hid her cash around her apartment until the first day of the month when her bills were due and the jar would once again be empty. James pocketed several quarters before re-thinking what he was doing and grabbed a haphazard handful of bills. James left the cramped apartment. He noticed heaps of over-stuffed black trash bags lined up along the tackily decorated hallway like hordes of soldiers lined up along the Great Wall.

"Trash day isn't Thursday. Our new neighbors are pigs," James exclaimed stepping widely over a very clearly used diaper and sliding almost comically on a rotting banana peel. "Look at all of this trash," he said leaning over the staircase rail peering down at the other hallways filled to capacity with waste all the way down to the ground level. "Diapers and cans and dried up food everywhere. Where are the garbage men? Is it a holiday? Are they on strike?" He tentatively made his way down the jam-packed staircase. As he went down, James noticed that all of the hallways were like Etna's, filled to capacity with refuse and teeming with unseen bacteria no doubt. Four flights down, James reached the lobby and struggled to push open the front door of the apartment building.

"Wonderful, it's a beautiful day." James breathed in as much fresh polluted city air as he could trying to get the horrible stench of so much garbage out of his nostrils. Every time he breathed in, the smell of decay and rot and death stuck to his nose hairs like glue. James set off on the five-block walk to Frankie's hoping Etna would give him a free lunch and, maybe if there was time before she goes back to work, do a bit of shopping and buy him something.

"-Allo, Love. 'Ow are you t'day? Shall we dine in our usual pub then, mate?" James rehearsed his phony British accent on his way to meet Etna.

He wished Etna could afford a cell phone so he didn't have to carry around so many quarters to call Simon all the time. James supposed he could help Etna out by asking his father for a chunk of his millions since he was always staying with her, eating her food and using his phony accent to con her into buying him stuff she couldn't afford. Or get a job. Then, reason overcame him as always, and he decided against begging his father for the right to breathe air yet again. James was, after all, Etna's "English Lover." Wasn't that more than enough to satisfy her?

James had walked the entire rubbish filled block before getting out of his own head and realizing, for a busy city like New York, he hadn't seen a single person, living, dead or undead. There were no cars whizzing past, no traffic, and no cranky middle-aged men in cabs honking in code to each other. The streets were oddly quiet and empty. Even the hulking buildings that towered over him looked decidedly different. They looked old and crumbling around their edges. He blinked several times. Was something wrong with his eyes? No, not his eyes. The city itself. What was wrong with this city, his city? Where were all of the people? The hustle and bustle of life teeming all around him? This troubled him. This didn't look like a street that was closed for repairs or a parade or a movie shoot. This was something different entirely. James couldn't remember a time in his life when he had ever felt this alone. He crossed the street without looking for traffic to use a phone booth. He thought hearing anyone's voice, even that of his bookie, would comfort him.

"Whoa, dude. What the Hell?" James jumped back from the phone booth when he realized there was already a man in there. "Get out! I need to make a call."

"I'm not leaving! This is my home. This is my home and I'm not going anywhere. This is my home. This is my home."

James stared at the old man chanting and rocking. The old man stared back.

"You live here?" He looked the elderly man up and down.

The man moved slightly to his left allowing James to see the inside of the phone booth. The entire phone booth was covered floor to ceiling, wall to wall, wallpapered in rubber duckies of all different sizes and variations. Some were wearing cute little sailor hats, others looked like ducky firemen. One was even wearing a fake string of plastic pearls plastered to its tiny yellow body. How were they held together? How did they stay on the wall? They couldn't just be stacked there. They would fall at the slightest sneeze if that were the case. There must have been a breeze because the man's pink bathrobe was opening in the wind showing the man's dirty faded boxer shorts.

James peered around the man's faded underwear and saw the whole booth was crammed with so much stuff that he couldn't see how the guy could even stand in there let alone live. James looked from the inside of the phone booth to the outside then inside and outside once again.

The man responded to James' previous question. "Yep, this is my home. Now you, sir, are trespassing. Go away." The look the vagabond gave James spoke for itself.

"You-you live here?" Still in shock over finding a man in a pink bathrobe living in a cramped phone booth in a world where he was the only person on Earth, James walked away. It was the only thing he could do. "Thanks," he called behind him as an afterthought. "I'll just find another one."

The man shouted after James shaking his head. "You won't find one that isn't occupied. You'll have to find another city to live in. I hear some places in Montana might have some available units." The man began to mutter to himself. "Man, kids today. Always trying to make it on their own and growin' up too fast." The man closed the hem of his pink robe in the phone booth door.

James quickened his pace, breaking out into a slight run. He hoped the homeless man wasn't following him. Seeing another human, even a crazy one, made him consider the possibility that he wasn't the last man on Earth. Given what he had just dealt with, this was only a semi-reassuring thought.

James ran his hand through his hair. "New York should really do something about the homeless population problem."

He came upon the intersection of 9th and Broadway. He spotted a phone booth, ran over to it and flung open the door dramatically. A mother was reading a fairy tale to her children. What could only be family photos lined the walls of the phone booth. He stared into the little boy's frightened eyes. James turned, ashamed he scared a small child, and sprinted off, taking the familiar route to Frankie's, wondering what was going on with the world.

He ran to the next phone booth and opened the doors without knocking, though he paused, thinking manners dictated he should. He found a middle-aged couple that spoke only angry French. Then the next- a family of mimes having a lunch worthy of any silent film. Then the next- a hulking man in a tutu with no teeth and a miniature poodle, also in a tutu. They were all the same. All of the phone booths were the same. Someone had created a home in every phone booth he stopped at, even the one outside of Frankie's Diner.

He went into Frankie's looking for something he couldn't place, humanity maybe, and a hot dog definitely. Just like Etna's apartment building and the street, Frankie's was empty. Not only empty but covered in a layer of decay and dust. No edible frankfurters here. James felt trapped in a world that shouldn't exist. He shouldn't exist.

James couldn't put his finger on it but he thought it quite odd that people would rather live in phone booths than in the multitude of abandoned homes around them. Each "person" he met had seemed wrong to him besides the fact they lived in a phone booth. As human as they looked, he wasn't sure if they really were.

James didn't know what to do. He ran back to the first phone booth. He didn't know why he chose that creepy old man, but he did, so that's where he went. It just felt right. The old man would be able to tell James what was going on. He hoped.

"So you're back, my boy. Didn't find anywhere to live did you? I told you, didn't I? Kids today just don't listen! The world is different today than it used to be. There's a guy three houses down who thinks he's dead. Course he ain't. That would be silly. But, he thinks he is all the same. Always walks around talking to himself about the day he died. Poisoned he says by his wife who is actually dead, by the way. Don't think she was poisoned though." The man stroked his beard, lost in thought.

"What?" Maybe coming to this man for help was a mistake. He wasn't making any sense talking to James about some guy who was dead but wasn't.

"Well, might as well come in out of the rain, boy. What's your name son?"

James walked in, staring up at the sky. There wasn't a cloud in sight. Rain drops rushed down on his face like a tidal wave. James blinked hard against the cold wet that invaded his being before walking in the phone booth.

"My name is James."

He looked around, surprised there was enough room in here for not only all of the stuff piled everywhere but for several more people to sit on the arm chairs or couches littering the vast space. James took a deep breath. Everything smelled like peppermints.

"Name's Mort. Sit, sit. I don't bite. Unless you're a fried fish that is."

James continued to stand, turning slowly in disbelief. The booths weren't made to be that big. You were just supposed to cram yourself in there and scrunch your elbows against your body to be able to make your call. You weren't supposed to be able to fit stuff in there. You're supposed to be able to barely stand still. You weren't supposed to be able to recline in a Lazy Boy. Somehow, now that speaking to this odd little man was his reality, he saw the booth and the world in a whole new light. He looked around noticing things he hadn't on his last visit.

James saw piles of clothes that were too small to fit Mort and a figurine of a tiny tuba so small it seemed like Barbie had finally chosen the profession of musician over her more industrious options like doctor or astronaut. Gum wrappers formed a series of chains turned into chintzy drapes hiding a small bedroom. Papers and books littered the space. He looked at some of the book titles. Anne Rice novels, OSHA Standards and Practices, *The Little Engine That Could*, *Gray's Anatomy* and *Things Fall Apart* were some amongst the eclectic collection. As he finally sat down on the couch, a musty stack of Green Lantern comic books toppled, splaying all over the floor of the phone booth.

"Why are people living in phone booths? The entire city is deserted. Why don't you all live in the buildings? All that stuff and space is just going to waste." James inquired of his strange host. Raising his arms above his head to recline further on the couch, his shirt raised just enough to show off a tattoo he got on a dare while drunk.

Mort noticed the purple and blue cartoon snake wrapped around the epsilon symbol made to look like Etna's name written in flowery cursive. "The Mark! You have the Mark!" Mort hugged himself rocking back and forth faster than he had when James first met him earlier that day. Mort seemed happy. Delirious even.

Like much of what Mort had said to him so far, James didn't understand Mort's most recent outburst. James looked all over the bare skin on his arms but couldn't find the mark Mort was so hyper about. Mort pointed to the same spot on James' shirt over and over. "My tattoo?" James lifted his shirt to show an old drunken mistake.

"You have the Mark of the Etna."

"The Mark of the Etna? Etna was my girlfriend's name. I only got the tattoo so I could get laid, man."

"Etna is no person. Etna is the largest planet in the Hellion Galaxy. It is, was, my home. There is a legend among my people of a Chosen One who was prophesized many blue moons ago to have the power to save our people from the Centurions, the very same alien race that overtook Earth many years ago. After this recent invasion, Etnans found out the prophecy was incorrect. Indeed there was not just one Chosen One but an army of Chosen Ones trained from birth by Queen Ladriss, all bearing the same mark you possess. Some of these soldiers were kept by her side. Some she sent here, unaware of their lineage, only knowing their mission subconsciously. You must have been sent here as a child, be-spelled to believe you were human to gather intel for our invasion. I can take you to the leaders who can remove the spell and make you remember who you really are. Do you want to wake up now?"

"No, this is crazy. I'm out. Have a nice life." Standing up to leave James bumped into a wall of rubber duckies. They didn't fall over. What were they held up with?

"Don't leave," Mort grabbed his arm to stop James from leaving. "You don't want to be out there at night. When it gets dark, bad things happen. These domes are the only thing that keep the bad away."

James stared into Mort's eyes, believing every word. There was a war brewing behind his eyes. James knew what he had to do. His brain didn't want to him to, though. James didn't want to chance his own life. He decided to trust his instincts not his brain. His gut had always gotten him out of trouble.

"Tell me more about this queen and her army deal you got going on." James switched seats so he was sitting on a fold-up chair next to a cardboard box filled with video tapes of the old television series Get Smart so he would be able to better hear Mort's story.

Well into the night, Mort told James the story of the Chosen One and Queen Ladriss' armies all bearing the Mark of Etna who rescued Etnans from the Centurions who devastated every planet they inhabited. Mort went on to tell James the story of the great war that happened many Etnan years ago, the enslavement and eventual genocide of the Centurions who James called the human race, and, finally, of the uprising of Etnans against the queen, creating a chasm so wide on Etna that it became uninhabitable, forcing those Etnans who were left to move to Earth. James looked up to where Mort pointed in the sky at where Etna should glow bright and light up the darkness. James realized Mort pointed to a round shadow where the moon should have been. The moon was still stuck in the sky, but it was too dark, casting deep shadows on the street. James saw where the bad things came from and why a phone booth would be safer than an apartment. The wind howled, rattling the phone booth doors. At least James hoped it was the wind and not something else, something unseen.

Mort bit his bottom lip, hard enough to draw strange blue blood, trying to think of a way to convince James to help his people reclaim their former glory and stop the unseen evil that plagued them ever since they moved to this desolate planet. James looked around the phone booth trying to avoid Mort's gaze by staring down a collection of naked troll dolls in the corner. He couldn't avoid the old man any longer. James looked into Mort's deep blue eyes, drowning in the pain and sadness that reflected back like the reflection of himself he saw in a pool of water he fell in the last time he was in Central Park.

"I'm ready." James couldn't believe what he was saying.

Mort and all of the other phone booth people he met earlier that day needed a hero, something to believe in. Everyone needs hope, even aliens from the moon. James decided right then and there that no matter how unqualified or inept to heroism he was, he was still going to help these people. He was still going to be their hope, their hero. They sat in silence watching the sun rise in all of its glorious emotion, angry red piercing the friendly oranges and cheery yellows. Mort shot James a look of approval, a phenomenal look of praise rivaling the sunrise they were experiencing, something you would only expect a proud father to give his son when he becomes a father himself.

"Are you ready to wake up?"

For more visit: jessicamathews.com

Swallow

Amy M. Zlatic

A great big whale swallowed Jonah. He turned out to be okay, though, after a few rough days. It all comes out in the end, right? That's my interpretation of the story. Besides, comparatively speaking, a whale swallowing a man isn't all that impressive. Whales are huge, after all, and people are relatively small. Jonah would have made a wicked x-ray, though.

People in street fairs swallow swords, but not really. They always pull them out again. That's disappointing, because they never get the x-ray. I knew a girl who was in circus school and she took a sword-swallowing class. I asked her how she was learning to do that, and she said, "Very slowly." She told me it's all a matter of overcoming your gag reflex, which sounds impressive but can be very dangerous if you're actually choking on something and the reflex doesn't kick in to expel. Her homework was to swallow a sword a little further each night. She was up to six inches or so the last I talked to her.

I've heard that sometimes people find it hard to swallow their pride. I've never understood that. I don't find it hard to swallow most anything.

Things I've swallowed to date:
- Fingernail clippers.
- A rubber band.
- A clip that keeps potato chip bags closed.

- A small screwdriver my dad used to tighten the arms on his glasses.
- One of my old Hot Wheels cars.
- A birthday candle. (Not lit, of course. That would be dangerous.)
- An undeveloped roll of film.
- A bouncy ball my dentist gave me when I was seven and had a good check-up. It was my favorite bouncy ball: a dull, swirly red, with extra rubber along the edge where the two halves of the mold fit together. If you bounced it just right it'd go flying off in unexpected angles. I like the unexpected.

The first time I swallowed something, I chose a small object. The whale swallowed a man, yes, but I am much smaller than a whale. I was five, and I ate a dime. It felt good going down. The ridged edges rolled right down my throat and I could feel the shiny silver disc sitting in my stomach. I chose a brand new dime, not one of those dark, crusty ones you find on the street. I have standards, you know. My mother freaked out when I told her. Lost her shit and called the pediatrician's exchange number because I told her when she was tucking me into bed for the night and it was too late to call the doctor's office. The triage nurse assured her that this was perfectly normal and that it should pass with no issues. She was right. It did. I didn't tell her anymore when I swallowed something. If it was that easy, there was no point in upsetting her.

I swallowed more coins, until that became boring. My dad would roll his eyes and shake his head, and my mother grew exasperated when they figured out what was going on. Her frantic responses dulled into resignation. She warned me about the germs on coins, and said that one of these days the money would get stuck and then I'd be in real trouble. So I moved on.

I liked rummaging through the junk drawer in the kitchen. All kinds of things get tossed in there, and most of them are quickly forgotten. I didn't forget them. I thought about them all day at school, musing about paper clips and errant screws and pen caps. I had to wait, though, until my sister finished her homework and moved on. Our parents always made us do our homework at the kitchen counter, where they could keep an eye on us and help us with any questions. I think they also wanted to monitor our internet time, because strange, dangerous threats lurk online, not in the kitchen junk drawer.

After dinner and homework, when the kitchen finally cleared out, I'd stand at the drawer, sifting through the treasures. My dad had stashed a fishhook in there. Did I dare? Nah. The delicate curve was fine, but that barb on the end just looked painful. No point in puncturing anything unnecessarily.

Things from the junk drawer I've swallowed to date:
• Batteries. I prefer AAs. They slide down easily and carry a lovely heft. Button batteries that go in watches and garage door openers are too much like coins, and far less interesting.
• A USB jump drive. I don't know what was on it. I thought it would have been great if my sister's homework was saved to it, because then she could have told her teacher, "My brother ate my homework." No one missed it, though, so it must not have carried anything important.
• Paper clips. Both large and small. My favorites are the ones coated in brightly-colored rubber; they remind me of M&Ms.
• A shell keychain that had "I went cocoNUTS in the Bahamas!" painted on it. I don't know where that came from as none of us has ever been to the Bahamas, but I sure know where it went.

What gave me up that time was the damn spoon. Bored with the junk drawer, I had pulled out the one next to it, the one that holds the flatware. Spoons look lovely, with curved, glinting surfaces and that comforting bowl that serves as a handy carrier at the end. It went down so easily, but wreaked havoc once it met its new neighbors in my bowels. I told my mother my tummy hurt, and after two days of insisting I just needed a good poop (she figured a coin finally got stuck, just as she had warned me), she took me to the doctor.

Those x-rays were beautiful. They were art. They belong in a museum somewhere, I think, my gorgeous creations. Some of the items that hadn't passed through yet, like the paper clips, got all bunched up together. I kind of wish I had slowed down on them, spaced them out better. The jump drive looked a little boring, mostly because it looked boring before I swallowed it. The spoon was lovely, clear as day. It looked much bigger on my x-ray than it did in the flatware drawer. The keychain was magnificent, every link between the shell and the ring clearly delineated. I wanted to paint "I went cocoNUTS in the Bahamas!" right on the x-ray. I could picture the little palm tree that sat jauntily next to the words.

The gastroenterologist called them "foreign objects" when he told my parents. I don't see them like that. Once they are in my belly, they are part of me. They aren't foreign any more. They are mine, and they are me. I studied my mother's face. She looked at me like I was a foreign object, which I found fascinating because I had once been in her belly. I failed to see the difference. My entry into her belly was simply by a different route.

My parents asked me over and over again why I swallowed these things. I couldn't answer them beyond shrugging, "I just like to." I am a straight-A student who plays youth soccer and baseball. I have friends. (Bonus: I have friends who also have kitchen junk drawers. It is like discovering the treasures of the Titanic over and over again when I am invited to sleep-overs.) I like how it feels. And I like knowing that I'm carrying things around inside, things no one else can get, things I don't have to share. My own little treasure chest. I mean, I know some of my treasures wind their way through and are eventually expelled, but they had to make quite a journey first. That's impressive.

After the procedure, I felt empty. My objects were gone. The doctor wouldn't give them back to me, even though I asked ten times before the sedation kicked in. I wonder where they went.

My parents cleaned out the junk drawer when we got home. I watched them looking around the kitchen, in between sneaking furtive glances at me. I heard my mother telling my sister she needed to count the flatware when she emptied the dishwasher. Clearly, I would need to be more sneaky. It's okay. I like a challenge. Since I was being watched like a hawk, I made a game out of it, and decided that I would try swallowing things that didn't belong to me. Well, they started off that way. Once they went down my throat, they were mine. All mine.

Other people's things I've swallowed to date:
- The tags off my dog's collar.
- The key to my dad's office.
- My sister's iPod Mini.
- My mother's favorite hair barrette.
- Grandad's pocket knife.
- A hamster-shaped Japanese eraser from the boy who sits next to me in class.

I wondered what would happen when things that belong to other people disappeared. It was my own little secret. I watched my classmate tear his desk apart looking for his eraser, knowing the whole time that it was in my belly. My treasures had a new, delicious secrecy.

I thought it was funny that even though my parents were watching me so closely, they never thought to ask me if I had seen their missing items. My sister took the blame for her missing iPod, despite her insistences that she didn't lose it, that she hadn't taken it to school and misplaced it for someone to steal. I guess because I took it off her nightstand and not from the junk drawer, my parents didn't think that it might be found in my stomach.

The second time my parents looked at the x-rays of my native objects (I refuse to call them foreign), they left the room to talk about what to do with me. I heard them whispering outside the door, confusion and sadness in my mother's voice and frustration in my father's. He seemed more concerned with the insurance company dropping our coverage since I kept pulling these stunts. I don't know why he called them stunts. I wasn't doing it for attention. In fact, I never even told anyone when I did it. If I wanted attention, I'd have said, "Hey, asshole, I just swallowed your office key!" I didn't say that, though. I didn't say anything while he tore apart his office bag and cursed my mother for losing yet another belonging of his.

A new doctor came into the room. The corners of her eyes crinkled when she talked to me, as she forced a smile during her questions. I didn't trust her, because she used my name too much. Every question had my name at the end, after a comma pause. I don't trust people who use names too much. Those people are either trying to make me understand that they are my friend (they are not) or they are desperately trying to remember my name (which they don't need, as they are not my friend). I answered her questions honestly, though, even while the name thing annoyed me. Was I abused? No. Was I unhappy? No. Did I ever think about taking my own life? No. What I was thinking about, during all this, was how much I wanted to try to swallow the pendant of her necklace. It had diamonds in it. I had never swallowed anything so expensive before. The iPod was pricey when my parents bought it, but it was a couple generations out of date by the time it showed up on an x-ray, so I don't really count that. I wondered if the diamonds would feel different going down. I made a note to myself to do a blind test, placing items of similar shape and size but different expense in a hat and then closing my eyes before choosing one to swallow. I bet I could tell what each one was, just like I had felt the dime's ridges the first time.

The gastroenterologist was out in the hall with my parents, explaining that he'd have to do yet another procedure to remove my larger treasures, the ones that wouldn't pass through on their own, but that he was convinced he could retrieve them all using an endoscopic procedure like the first time. My mother wondered how I had gotten the bigger things down. I heard him laugh, "You'd be amazed at what a person can swallow!" I glanced out the door in time to see my mom turn green. I didn't find it funny, and I didn't see it as disgusting, so I really didn't understand either one of them.

I promised the doctor I wouldn't swallow anything else, because I thought that's what she wanted to hear, and the gastro prepped me for surgery. As the anesthetic kicked in, I began to dream. I dreamed about people swallowing swords, and of the great whale swallowing a whole man, and what diamonds would look like on an x-ray, and of what else I could find to swallow once I got home.

When I woke up, I was in a room where there weren't any objects to swallow. I have lots of friends here, too, and sometimes we get to go out on the front lawn and play whiffle ball. Private tutors come and go, but they always take my pens, pencils and erasers with them when they leave, so my homework consists mostly of studying my books. My monitors sit with me at meals, and collect and count my utensils just as soon as I've finished dessert. I keep looking around for things to swallow, but everything here is just so big. I guess I will have to study, like my friend in circus school, and work on something large each night. I wonder what I can find.

FINAL DAYS OF SUMMER

Wanda L. Lovan

Hummingbirds glitter like jewels
As the weather cools
And folks close their pools.
Kids head for schools
With new writing tools
Autumn beauty almost knocks us off our stools,
Before the arrival of witches and ghouls!

As we head toward the Autumnal Equinox
Blackbirds gather in flocks,
Hummingbirds fight
And savor each bite.
The wind blows,
We hear the cawing of the crows
As the summer activity slows.

The next season brings gentle breezes
Accompanied by fewer sneezes.
As the blossoms decrease,
Painted Lady butterflies
Compete with Monarchs
Soon to be Central America bound
And no longer in Missouri found.

Tropical storms
Create butterfly swarms
On nearby farms
And students flock to the dorms
Weather cools and warms
And dew forms.

Waning corn moon peers through the cloud
Stridulating cicada symphony is very loud
As I water my plants
After donning long pants
Avoiding mosquitoes with dental implants.
Each season
Has a reason!

BREAD DAY

Evelyn Buretta

in a grey crock bowl with yeast and warm water
she dumped handfuls of flour
beat all with the rhythm of her migraine
its source the handsome man she married
for love not the harshness of life
on an isolated farm with a stoic husband
who worked the land to squeeze money
out of wheat and beans and corn

she released her tension
when the sticky dough bulged
by punching pounding
walloping whacking and smacking
that white mass into mounds
scooped them into pans
four in one and two in the other for him
and her brood of six screeching kids

she stoked the kindling
in the wood-burning stove
waited for the second rising
peeled potatoes canned tomatoes
boiled diapers squeezed lemons
cut green beans fried sausage
sliced strawberries and knew
the moment to slide the smooth loaves

into the just-right temperature
and when to remove those golden heaps
of goodness that sent a scent
through the house then plopped
her prizes on the kitchen table
and hoped for a morsel of praise

Man at the Crossroads

Brad R. Cook

I sat at a dusty crossroads waiting for whatever came my way. Fate was taking a little longer than usual that day. The world shifted out of focus and blurred my vision. Then strolling along the western road, the Devil walked on a mission. A perfect waist and impeccable taste. He's the type people rush online to rate, like a lawyer your mother wants you to date.

Draped in the finest silk suit style, he reached out his bronzed hand with a shiny smile. I shook it out of courtesy because my mother taught me right, but when he tried to yank my soul, I pulled him in real tight. "What is it you need? Why intercede?"

"No loophole, I'm here for your soul."

"You'll never succeed. You can't feed my greed."

"It's dreams I adore. I come bearing contracts, money, and more."

Suddenly surrounded, every fan astounded. Each with a book from my mind awaiting to be signed. Everything I ever wanted... the vision left me haunted.

"My soul you will not reap. For undaunted, I will not sleep until you realize... my price is not cheap.

He challenged me with a test that sounded bizarre – to rock the greatest song on the electric guitar. I shrugged and said, "no way. I can't even play."

He asked if I could fiddle, and I said, "not even a little."

He challenged me to sing a tune

unrehearsed, but my voice was harsh from thirst. A tribute song would sound wrong, so I told him to go away, for a year and a day. He did not play along, and crossed his arms to prove he's strong.

The Devil wanted to devour my soul, but I refused his every toll. An explosion of fiery lies burned within his eyes. I caught that horned-demon studying me, with a wicked grin he thought I didn't see.

"I challenge you to write the greatest tale ever told." He announced by reading a scroll.

I looked him square in one eye and asked, "Poetry or prose?"

"Either," he said as if loving my woes.

And with a sweet angelic tone, I asked, "word count?"

"Keep it short," he sneered, as if tallying the amount.

I wrote until my fingers began to cry and used my blood when the pen went dry. Every word laid down in perfect order, no editor need horde over.

With confidence, I handed him a page of allegory, a one of a kind short story.

His beady eyes align, darting over every line, pondering each word like a fine wine, as if studying a tome at an ancient shrine. The Devil read it thrice times nine, and growled, "You had help from the divine!"

He cast the paper to the ground, which cracked, and fire rose all around. Without a word he did retract, by covering himself in a shroud of black. He disappeared in a mini mushroom cloud, and I picked up the paper to read the words aloud. "I sat at a dusty crossroads…"

For more, visit: bradrcook.com

Patient Zero

Joshua Skurtu

In 2013, at the height of the financial crisis, a new pathogen broke out among the populace. It started with one person, patient zero. This is his story.

The medical center building sat near a freeway off-ramp among a row of mini-malls. The building seemed cold and sterile, with a short pile carpet leading onto cheap tile flooring. The walls were void of any art or decor, instead layered with a two-tone muted mix of brown and purple. The colors would never excite any patients to any sort of insanity.

John Palmer sat in the doctor's office. Among the first symptoms, John suffered from a severe lack of appetite and no desire to drink any fluids. His wife had pushed him to make the appointment. Due to John's obesity, his physician initially suspected an endocrine disorder.

"Middle age. Overweight. Most likely diabetes," Doctor Pring said. She pushed a loose strand of her black hair behind her ear and absentmindedly chewed on a pen. She wore a white lab coat and made limited eye contact, staring at the laptop screen for most of the exam.

"Diabetes," John repeated. "I thought diabetes made people eat all the time."

"Not exactly. And sometimes a side-effect of diabetes is what is called gastroparesis. The high blood sugar damages the nerves in the stomach and fails to send the messages to the brain correctly. Hence the lack of hunger."

"I guess that makes sense."

"We'll take some blood samples at the lab to confirm. I'll need you to abstain from eating anything for six hours before the test."

"How much is this going to cost?" John asked.

"The tests aren't much, but diabetes can cost you an arm and a leg if it isn't treated. Literally."

"I don't have health insurance."

Dr. Pring gave a forced smile that looked more like a cringe. "I get that a lot these days. We'll work something out. We always bill the insurance companies ten times what it costs. So most providers will give you a reasonable discount if you don't have insurance. It'll still cost a pretty penny to treat the diabetes, but the alternative is death."

John provided his blood the next day and went home to wait. After a week the results came back. All the laboratory results showed negative. He didn't have diabetes and he didn't have gastroparesis.

By then, John could no longer eat or drink. He neither had the desire or the compulsion to do either. He stopped urinating after three days and failed to defecate after only a single day. His cessation of these basic human necessities failed to affect him in any reasonable manner. He felt no fatigue. He could still move and function, despite the starvation and dehydration conditions. He even continued his regular regime, including exercise at the gym and tennis on Saturday morning.

"You haven't eaten or drank all week?" Doctor Pring sounded worried.

"I ate part of a granola bar five days ago and I took a sip of water four days ago, but I spit it out."

"Why would you do that?"

"It tasted bad. I mean, it tasted like water, but the taste of water itself repulsed me. So I spat it out."

John sat on the edge of the examination table,

dangling his feet while they spoke. Doctor Pring made more eye contact during this visit. Her eyes remained wide and she shook her head as if disagreeing with a conversation only she could hear.

"If you go too long without water, you will die. I'm surprised you aren't exhibiting signs of dehydration. Do you feel tired?"

"No."

Dr. Pring lifted up the back of John's shirt and placed the cold stethoscope on his back. "Big breath. And release." She removed the device and did the same up the front of his shirt. "Your lungs sound fine, if a little wheezy, but nothing to worry about. Heart is strong. No physical distress. You honestly have me stumped Mr. Palmer. I want you to see a gastroenterologist. That's a stomach doctor. He'll be able to tell us what's going on inside your belly, but we can't rule out a neurological disorder. I want you to see a neurologist for that."

"Is he like a shrink?" John asked.

"No. A neurologist deals with diseases of the brain, spine, and nerves. We need to cover this on all sides if we want to catch this before it gets too bad."

Referrals in hand, John returned home to his family. John and his family had lost their health insurance after John's employer laid him off. The few visits to the doctor and the emergency room earlier this year already racked up thousands of dollars in bills in his name. Thousands that he and his family could not pay. John tossed the referrals on the nightstand and they stayed there for days. He couldn't rationalize going to more visits when he felt fine. He wasn't eating, but he also wasn't bleeding out of his anus or crawling to the toilet every few hours to vomit.

It was a financial decision to stop treatment. His wife Jennifer fought him on the decision. They sat together at the dinner table with the stacks of bills split into different categories. Necessities made up the first stack. Things like electricity, food, rent. Most of the bills that dominated the second stack were things like cable television, internet, a credit card they used for eating out at restaurants, and other non-essentials. The third stack were items they had already decided to toss in the garbage in an attempt to forget about them. At the top of that stack were John's medical bills and the referrals.

"We have to prioritize." John held up the first stack and set it in front of Jennifer. "We have to feed our children. We have to keep the house over their head. We need to be able to provide heat and running water. These we have to find a way to pay."

"It's summer, John," Jennifer said. "We don't need heat. And your health should be a part of that stack."

"Going to the doctor might never help whatever I have. I don't feel sick or anything and I'm sure I'll eventually be able to eat again. We have to wait it out and see what happens. For all we know, I'm already on the road to recovery." John picked up an apple from the fruit bowl at the end of the table. He stared at it for a long while and then tried to take a bite, but stopped after sinking his teeth in. It seemed like a normal apple, but the concept of apple seemed lost to John. The apple seemed like something disgusting to him now, like feces or vomit. He stared at it and felt revulsion as if it were teeming with maggots

"Most treatments use the body's ability to heal itself anyway." John set the apple back in the bowl. "I never really liked apples." John let out a big breath and then looked up at his wife. "The treatments only make you more comfortable. Medical bills go in the trash for now. We can afford a few bills from the second stack, as long as they are important."

John picked up the cable television bill and read it.

"We pay $100 a month for TV?" John asked. "We can definitely do without that."

"It's summer. The kids are home all day. What else are they going to do? They'll drive me up a wall if they can't watch cartoons."

"We can get an antenna. That's still television," John said.

"Does that even work any more?"

"I think so," John said. "That's all we had when we were kids. My older brothers always made me stand up and hold the antenna to boost the signal, but it worked."

After a few hours, the trash stack had grown, and the stack they intended to pay had slightly risen. Jennifer held onto the medical bills, pushing the point, but John knew it wouldn't work. They had two children together and all the money they had went to food and other necessities. Food was cheap; Health care was expensive. It was a rational argument that Jennifer fought him on, but conceded after John made the case for their starving children.

"Won't somebody think of the children?" John said in a shrill southern belle accent.

By the end of that first week, John lost even the need to sleep.

John noticed that he wasn't sleeping. He would lie down in bed next to his wife, stare at the ceiling for hours, and then get up and wander around the house. At first, he turned on the television. He watched a few late-night talk shows, a few infomercials, but no amount of boredom seemed to tire him. In the past, he could always cure insomnia with one of the worst infomercials of all time. It starred a man with greased-back hair and a collared shirt selling kitchen gadgets that no one could ever possibly need, such as a full-sized rotisserie, a set of pans that used the heating power of magnets, and even a set of knives endorsed by a fitness guru. John followed this plan for a few nights, but he found that when he got bored with the shows he still couldn't sleep. His mind would instead wander and he would end up ignoring the television.

After he gave up on television as a sleep aid, he tried to read. But no matter how long and drawn out the novel *Ulysses* was, his eyes remained wide. Any boredom only translated into becoming lost in a thought mid-paragraph and being unable to finish even a single page. He tried exercising, but even that couldn't exhaust him to sleep. He drove to the gym and went to every piece of exercise equipment in the building. He did cardio. He did weight lifting. He even tried doing some yoga followed by deep meditation. None of it tired him, and he didn't even feel physically exhausted. Sleeping pills didn't make him drowsy at all. Every night after he fought to tire himself, he returned to bed, sometimes past sunrise, and continued his ceiling gazing. He didn't feel sad or angry or anxious. He felt nothing. He simply could not sleep.

Jennifer confronted him about it on the tenth day. She waited until the children were at school.

"Have you been having trouble sleeping?"

John stared at the wall, sitting up to the kitchen table. He didn't have any food in front of him, but he sat with Jennifer while she ate. When he failed to respond, Jennifer touched his shoulder and repeated the question.

"Have you been sleeping well?"

John looked up into her blue eyes. She wore a pair of sweat pants and an old Aerosmith t-shirt. She blew a strand of her curly blond locks out of her face while she spoke to him.

"I haven't slept in five days."

"Five days?" Jennifer sounded alarmed.

"At least. I know for sure it has been five days. It could be longer. I haven't eaten or drank anything close to eight days."

"That's not possible. I'm sure you slept some. I noticed you gone a few times, but you go to bed when I do."

John shook his head and resumed staring at the wall. It wasn't that he was avoiding eye contact with his wife. He loved her very much. He simply felt an impulse to let his gaze wander. An urge he couldn't quite understand.

"The world record for going without sleep is 11 days. That's not even possible without a massive amount of stimulants."

John shook his head again and shrugged.

After another week without sleep, Jennifer begged him to see a doctor. It was then that the tremors began. When he reached for a knife in the kitchen his hand shook violently. It moved down his arm to his chest to the point where his whole body shook as if he were a contestant in an all-night dance-a-thon, spasming to an unheard beat. He found Jennifer in the den that afternoon whispering into her cell phone.

"Who are you calling?" John sat down, holding onto the armrest. This started another one of the tremors. It traveled up his right arm, but he grabbed it with his left and it subsided.

"I'll talk to you later," Jennifer said into the receiver. "No one important."

"You're cheating on me!" John held up one finger in the air in a comical manner, like a detective that had solved the big case. Any levity the attempt at humor might have brought to the situation was immediately lost when the finger in the air started to tremble.

"That's exactly what I'm doing." Jennifer ignored the tremor and looked down at the floor. "I've been sleeping with that oil billionaire that killed your twin brother after he seduced me in the hospital while you were recovering from your amnesia."

"I knew it! I just couldn't remember it!" John put his hands in his lap and clasped them together as if to ward off an incoming tremor. "We watch way too many soap operas."

"We'll worry about that when we're employed." Jennifer smiled and brushed John's shoulder with her fingers. "I love you, John. I'm scared."

"Who was that for real on the phone?"

"Do you honestly want to know?"

"Yes."

"I've been calling doctors. Trying to find someone that will treat you for free. All the non-profits say we made too much money this year. Apparently, you have to be broke for a long time before they will help."

"Yeah."

"But I started calling doctors directly. Hoping someone might do a case study on your illness in return for treatment."

"Any takers?" John asked.

"None so far. But I found a journalist that wants to write a story about you."

"Oh, come on!" John gripped the armrests and looked away. He turned back with something else to say. "You want me to be a sideshow? How will that help? You want my story to be on the 5-o'clock, right after the city's murder report and right before weekend weather report?"

"It might help."

"How?"

"Maybe someone knows what you have and they see the story." Jennifer put her hand on top of John's on the armrest. "Maybe a doctor will hear about it and want to help. It won't be on television. It's a reporter from the newspaper."

"Oh, that's nice," John said, sarcastically. "If it's in the newspaper, I'm sure of the seven geriatrics that still read it, one of them will be an award-winning neurologist that can fix me right up."

"They publish online too. I read it every day."

Man Stays Awake for Weeks, No Food / Drink. That was the title of the article. John scanned the article, noticing the journalist had misrepresented a few of the facts. The story stated that doctors continued to study him, even though he hadn't seen a physician in weeks.

The third week, John started wandering through the neighborhood at night. He felt more alive in the warm night air of summer instead of being cooped up in front of a television. He didn't have any goal or destination in the wandering. He simply wanted to walk. At first, John circled the block a few times, staring off into the darkness. After a few laps, he decided to change direction. He didn't want any of his neighbors to notice him wandering around in front of their homes. He's not a stalker. He decided to pick a direction and keep walking. He walked through the subdivision, made it out to the first gas station near the row of restaurants on 10th street, turned left onto Washington Avenue and kept walking. By the time the sun rose, John found himself standing on the side of the road next to a field of corn.

John stopped in his tracks. He looked around. The road laid empty except for John and a few empty cans on the side. He looked down and saw his feet. When he first started the walk, he didn't know how long he would be out. He had left the house wearing only a raggedy pair of flip-flops. Through the night they had fallen or torn off and John's bare feet stood exposed on the asphalt. Blood and scabs peeked out from the sides of his feet, the tips of his toes worn off from dragging through the street.

When John returned, he wrapped his feet in some gauze and peeked into the bedroom. Jennifer was still in bed. In the pale morning light, she rested on her side, with only her shoulder exposed beneath the plush white comforter. John bent down over her to kiss the back of her shoulder. That was when it happened. For the first time in weeks, he felt an urge. He didn't immediately recognize the urge. It had been so long. John sniffed her shoulder and the urge increased. She rolled over to find him hovering over her and smiled up at him.

"You feeling frisky?" She pulled him down by his collar and kissed him.

John leaned back and looked into her eyes. He couldn't remember the last time they made love. It was his husbandly duty, so he smiled and kissed her again. She pulled him down on top of her and they rolled across the bed, with Jennifer ending up on top.

John leaned forward and kissed her stomach. He could smell her scent, the saltiness with a hint of perfume. The fleshy sides of her breasts looked inviting. Even more than usual. John imagined a feeling of being full. He felt so empty all of a sudden as if he had not eaten in a week. He felt a need to fill himself, but he could not quite grasp what that meant. He felt ravenous and a hunger overwhelmed him. His kiss on her left breast turned into a snarl. He drooled at a whiff of her scent. Images of torn flesh and gnashing of teeth scattered his mind. Without another moment's hesitation, he bit into the meat of her breast and drew a stream of blood across the white bedding. The blood filled his mouth, yet the flesh itself remained attached.

Jennifer screamed. She flung her entire body back, dislodging John's teeth from her skin. John pushed himself back, a tear of blood running down both sides of his mouth. John stood up to stop her. Instinct told him to block her escape, but when he saw her face of absolute horror, when he saw her hold a pillow out to ward him off, he realized what he had done.

"What did you do?" Jennifer yelled and grabbed at the wound on her exposed breast. "You bit me!"

John reached out to console her. "I'm sorry..."

Jennifer took a step back and swung the pillow across his path. She looked around to find an escape and then reached behind her and picked up a lamp.

"Stop!" John backed away and pushed his way through the door behind him. He grabbed his clothing as he went. He rushed through the living room, out the front door, down the street, and tried to not look back. He didn't want to hurt his wife and he didn't feel like he had control over that decision. He didn't understand what had happened. He only knew he couldn't trust himself near her right now.

For more, visit: JoshuaSkurtu.com

The Mechanical Mansion of Reginald Porter

Jennifer Stolzer

The Porter Mansion watched the street from behind a broad garden. Inside was exactly what Bonnie Cartright was looking for: a stable position, good pay, room and board, and uniforms provided. Most importantly, it was the home of robotics pioneer Reginald Porter. Bonnie's heart skipped in an irregular beat as she marched up the steps to her new employment carrying nothing but the signed paper from her "father" confirming his consent. The head housekeeper didn't suspect a thing.

The building was everything its reputation boasted. Elegant dark wood furniture, gold-leafed accents, and décor older than the empire cluttered every inch of wall space, gathering cobwebs and dust so stubborn it could have been part of the design. Paintings of Porters past and present lined the many wallpapered halls. There were railroad men, magicians, inventors... John Porter, Reginald's father, was on nearly every surface. The one Porter missing was Reginald, the last living of his illustrious line. He was a mysterious figure, rarely seen except on paper and heir to a great fortune. For a while he was declared the town's most eligible bachelor, but that title, while fact, was largely a joke. Reginald never saw anyone, especially not suitors. After his father's death, his hermitage only worsened. Instead of locking himself in his house, he locked himself in a single room. The staff could not address him in person or enter his chamber while he was present, which was every day and at all hours. Each morning instructions were left on the door; the only evidence that the man really existed. The staff gossiped that Reginald was actually a ghost, but Bonnie believed he was alive. She had to after traveling so long and so far.

There was a time the Porters were the talk of the town. Genius and inventor, Reginald's father, John, pioneered steam and electric power, knowledge of which he passed on to his innovative son. The town hall still ran on the generator Reginald built for them. Other contraptions – the riverless mill, the ice-making machine, the kinetic tower – put the city on the map. No one had ever seen such creative application of scientific principles, but that was five years ago, before John Porter's death. The notable inventor was killed in a lab explosion on the third floor of the mansion. Reporters at the time said that Reginald was also harmed in the accident. Every newspaper said he kept his face hidden at all times by a hat and coat.

Bonnie's fascination with the Porters began shortly after the accident. She read every article and report published about them going back decades. She was particularly interested in Reginald. He was an endlessly generous man, giving away inventions and solving problems in his community. There were no officially documented pictures of him, not even at his father's funeral. Bonnie knew better. She'd bribed the archivist at the newspaper for a chance to look at the negatives of a photo taken at the graveside. There, on the hill as John was laid in the plot beside his wife, was a man in the same long coat and wide-brimmed hat reported after the explosion. Reginald Porter was always there, if you had a powerful enough microscope and knew where to look.

To the general public, the mansion was Reginald Porter's real face. Important friends and dignitaries often called on Mr. Porter. They never saw their host, but were taken by the automated tools and contraptions on display in his home. Bonnie thought the clockwork and electronic knicknacks looked more likely to complicate human activities than to help them. She could spot a stain on the carpet and scrub it up in minutes, whereas the carpet-cleaning robot used seven limbs and two hours to clean the whole rug whether it was stained or not. The curtain-cleaning robots were the same; they understood simple commands, but they didn't take direction like a human worker would. The most successful of the inventions was the robot Macaw in the dining room china cabinet, and that was only because it was impractical by design. Bonnie could feel it watching her from the other side of the glass. She got the impression it knew secrets it lacked the ability to tell.

As a maid, Bonnie was expected to share a room with seven other hired girls. Lights-out was at exactly ten o'clock every night. No girls were to leave the bunks after lights-out, not even to use the bathroom. Bonnie took off her black slippers, but kept her uniform on as she waited beneath the blankets for the housekeeper's lamp to pass on its nightly rounds. It flashed through the northern door, then flashed again in the southern door. Bonnie closed her eyes and waited for the housekeeper's door to click shut before slipping quietly out.

Reginald's private chambers were on the third floor of the mansion. Bonnie's ticking heart stuttered as she padded on stocking feet through the shrouded hallways, careful to avoid the dining room with the watchful bird, and the windows where the yard-tending robots worked day and night on the garden. She didn't bring a lamp, and avoided patches of moonlight on her way up to the second floor. This was where the family used to live, back when John and his wife Amelia were alive. There wasn't a lot available in the archives about Amelia Porter, only that she was wealthy and more than a little eccentric. She died with Reginald's birth – a tragedy in the modern era. If they had taken her to a hospital it might have been prevented, but the Porters were old-fashioned and Amelia was afraid of people. Physicians suspected that the death was caused by a blood condition that Reginald inherited, resulting in his seclusion. Psychologists surmised health was not an issue, and that over-protection from John or the lack of motherly attention caused Reginald to grow into an agoraphobic hermit. Bonnie doubted these guesses and harbored resentment toward the men responsible. What business was it of theirs why Reginald was the way he was? Throughout his whole life, people had tried to figure him being out without him present. The only way to know a man was to talk to him in person. Face to mysterious face.

Bonnie was careful to climb the third-floor steps close to the wall to avoid creaking. Only the housekeeper was allowed to the top of the building. She was the oldest and most loyal of the maids in the house, and had worked for the family when John and his wife were both alive. As such, she was the only one trusted so close to Reginald's private space. But the housekeeper was asleep, which is why it gave Bonnie a start when a figure crossed the hall at the top of the stairs.

Bonnie flattened herself to the wall, praying not to be seen. The figure at the top continued its path into an adjacent room. Its footsteps were heavy and forceful, like someone dropping a lead weight over and over. Bonnie slid along the wallpaper until she reached the topmost landing and was able to peer through the open doorway. The room was a study with a full library and antique desk covered in papers and notebooks. The figure clanked around out of view, shuffling things. Bonnie crawled to the threshold and bent her head in an awkward but covert effort to see.

The figure was a full-body automaton. Its copper limbs appeared almost skeletal on their flimsy ball-joint and cable mechanisms. It had a translucent glass head and a bulbous cylindrical metal chest that whirred and squeaked with unseen clockwork. The robot's movement relied on a barely controlled fall. It moved in jerks and stops and landed heavily on every step. The automaton reordered books on the shelves and straightened a couple picture frames before turning in place. Bonnie slipped out of view as it exited to the hall. She could feel the rattle of its footfalls through the floorboards as it headed away, leaving the smell of burning metal and the telltale clank of Porter robotics in its wake. Bonnie followed at a safe distance while it putt-putted about straightening things, and gathering bits of paper and different books from the various rooms.

Reginald's private chambers were at the end of the hall where John Porter's laboratory used to be. The door was newer than the others in the hall, with a chalkboard sign hanging from a nail at eye-level. The board was clean, most likely wiped by the housekeeper after receiving Reginald's daily instruction. Bonnie waited for the robot to clatter out of sight and measured the distance in long, careful strides. She brought a knuckle to the door and knocked.

There was no answer. She risked raising her voice a fraction and trying again. "Mr. Porter?"

The silence beyond was broken by the clunk of the robot approaching. Bonnie hustled herself into the nearest closet and closed herself inside as it entered the hall. The robot clanked and sputtered toward her door. Bonnie held perfectly still with her hand on the knob. The automaton was on the other side, emitting steam and a steady wooshing she couldn't hear from a distance. A strong oil and kerosene smell wafted through the crack as she risked a peek between the hinges.

The robot was facing Reginald Porter's bedroom. A pile of books had appeared on the nearby table along with a bit of chalk that the robot reached for with its pincer-like hand. The robot grasped the white stick delicately in its claw and with a jerking motion of its whole body, scribbled lines on the slate. Task complete, it put the chalk in the table's only drawer and drew the portal open. The robot lifted the books in both hands, entered the room, and sealed the door behind itself with the soft click of a deadbolt.

Bonnie poked her head out of the closet to read the robot's message:

Be attentive to the pictures. Purchase more ink.

Bonnie pressed her lips tight and dashed as fast as she could back to her bed. Details from her research reordered themselves in her head as she lay sleeplessly. The next day she did her chores and performed duties with one ear listening for stomping footsteps upstairs.

The automaton repeated its rounds the next night, although the benign tidying didn't seem to follow a pattern. It opened a couple windows, watered the plants, and sat in the moonlight so long Bonnie thought it might have shut down. The limbs were controlled by a series of wires and pullies. The head was glass and vaguely human, as if the features were sculpted with a poker while the rest was still warm. An odd cylinder-like a music box was tucked up in the skull – she could see its silhouette backlit by the moonlight as spider-like legs pedaled in steady rhythm. When twilight broke it geared back up and marched off to Reginald's bedroom.

The note it left on the door read *'Be more diligent with the plants.'*

Bonnie sneaked upstairs every night that week, but the automaton didn't come out again. Reginald's door remained shut with a blank slate hanging slightly askew on its peg. After seven days, Bonnie's impatience overtook her. She rose before midnight and with a heartbeat ticking in time with the old the grandfather clock, climbed the stairs to the third floor and marched up the hall. The sign on the door was still blank. The world around her still silent. Bonnie pressed her ear to the wood to listen, but there were no mechanical sounds. The door creaked on its hinges.

Not locked. Had it ever been? Bonnie's heart

remained steady as she swung the panel inward. The space beyond was open and airy – far from the exploded ruins or the dusty neglect professed by the newspaper experts. The space had polished floors, painted walls, and wide open windows facing the countryside. There was a phonograph, a piano, a balcony conservatory caged in glass around an indoor garden growing herbs.

In the far corner was a workbench covered in trinkets. Bonnie recognized the telltale elements of Porter design – electric batteries, switch boxes, pullies and cables, mechanical arms – as well as the glass shape sitting in the center.

The robot's glass head stared at her with its suggested eyes. The music box-type device that was once inside lay before it with pieces scattered in perfect lines across a white silk. Beside it, half-drawn diagrams of its internal structure lay weighted by faceted glass. A splotch of ink marred the delicate line work with one drop trailing like a tear from its heart. Still wet.

Bonnie's feet froze mid-step, mind flipping through her theories in the cast of the lifeless glass eyes. She considered escape when the door behind her closed with the soft deadbolt click. She turned to see the robot standing before her without its head.

Bonnie suppressed a scream and stumbled back. The robot teetered a moment. A puff of steam hissed from its clockwork chest as it stepped forward. Bonnie threw one hand up on reflex. "Stop!"

The robot obeyed. It set its foot back down and wobbled stiffly as its weight settled into place. She noticed it was carrying a sheet of clean paper in one hand. Over its shoulder was a coat rack with a long black coat and a hat.

Bonnie lowered her arm. "Are you Reginald Porter?"

The robot shifted again, venting more steam. The gears in its chest clicked at accelerated speed. It raised one hand, palm flat as if directing her to wait, then hissed and clanked across the room to the work bench. Bonnie watched as its two-fingered hands fit the disassembled music box back together with delicate precision. It fit the glass dome that was its head over the box and locked it. With a shudder, placed the combination back between its shoulders. Something clanged within its cylinder chest followed by a patter of tiny clicks. Pulleys drew the robot's arms back to its sides and it turned toward her again. A musical tone rang within its blown glass head.

"Yesssssssssssssssssss."

Was this from the accident? An imitation of life? On the wall was the first and only picture of Reginald Porter she had ever seen – the death photo of an infant child laying beside his mother in a casket. There never was a son. This creature was Reginald. It had been since the day it was "born."

The gears in the robot clicked like typewriter keys. The music box turned again, creating a deep tone like a man's voice with the crackle of automation. "Why are.... you.... here?"

Bonnie shook herself back to the present. Nothing had changed. She extended her hand. "Mr. Porter. I'm Bonnie Cartright. I've come a long way to find the famous inventor."

The robot, Reginald, adjusted his posture to appear slightly more at ease. It bent its hips so that its head turned to one side. "John... Porter... is... dead."

"Not John, sir. You." She kept her hand outstretched. "Reginald. The man responsible for the robots in this very famous house."

Reginald shifted again, drawing attention to the death photos. "You... accept... my... self."

"You're not alone, Mr. Porter. We knew something special was happening here," Bonnie stepped forward and took his metal hand in her own. "I've been looking all over for someone with robotic skill and intelligence. I never thought I'd find both creator and creation in one, but I'm glad I did."

She untied the bow in her apron strings and lay the

white lace on the workbench, then unbuttoned the collar of her black uniform dress.

"Wha... at?" Reginald staggered.

Bonnie pulled open her dress to reveal the edge of the pale silicone cowl that served as skin for her face, shoulders, and neck. Beneath it, the metal frame and fabric coating of her real body hid the softly whirring centrifuges and clockwork mechanisms beneath. She drew open a panel at the center of her chest and showed the robot her heart. It was a steel and copper creation with a winding key at the center. The head of the key had snapped, lodging the teeth in the complex mechanics beneath. She felt it shudder within her as the driver ground against the twisted metal. "Mr. Porter. I need someone who can fix me. My creators couldn't do it, not without removing the heart and killing me. I need a genius to find a solution, or I will become a simple doll."

Reginald stood unmoving. It was impossible to tell what he was thinking.

Bonnie stepped toward him again. "Please, Mr. Porter. I am willing to pay."

Reginald's arm rose. Bonnie shut her eyes and waited for him to reach into her chest, but instead a metal finger brushed the apple of her cheek.

"Face..." the music box voice sounded sadder somehow. "Skin."

"I can give them to you," she said. "My creators invented a chemical substance they pour into a mold. They can help your limbs and movement as well, they are good at that. Everything but the heart. They don't understand the heart."

"You... understand," Reginald said. "We...are... alive."

"We are alive." Bonnie counted the tick in her chest. "For me... only with your help."

Reginald cleared the books and drawings away. Bonnie sat, then lay, so that he may begin to work.

The next morning, a young woman and an old man boarded a coach. The girl was dressed as a house maid. The man wore a long coat and a wide-brimmed black hat. The house remained open, the robots all hard at work. Speculation about the fate of Reginald Porter found resurgence but no one ever knew the truth about where he'd gone. Somewhere, inside a china cabinet, the mechanical Macaw blinked, and saw.

For more, visit: jenniferstolzer.com

Shaking the Tree
A Bree MacLeod Story

Jennifer Lynn

Bree MacLeod's fingers traced slow circles around the hide of her Walton's bodhrán. Her gaze softened as her eyes tracked the thin wisps of smoke, spiraling gently skyward from the incense burning on the altar before her. She had lit it as an offering, a gift to honor the Sacred. She breathed in its musky scent and a door cracked open within her.

"Blessed is the Mystery," she whispered.

The droning from the hide washed through her. Closing her eyes, she exhaled and settled more deeply into the cushion she used for client journeys. As her eyes slowly opened, her gaze drifted over the wooden rim of her drum and she considered the woman seated opposite her. Shadows spilled across the petite frame, obscuring the contours and details of the round face.

Daphne, Bree reminded herself mentally. *Daphne O'Shea.*

"Hunted."

The word reverberated from the Otherworld and ached through Bree. Her breath caught in her throat and she forced herself to inhale.

"Let it be, mo Ghrá… my Love," a voice—feminine, ancient, loving—rippled through Bree. *"Come… Let the waters carry you."*

Bree smiled as the resonant voice of the goddess Bríghid, her Otherworldly Teacher and the mother of her lineage, echoed and dissolved into the droning of the drum. The low, moaning sound reverberated through Bree and her body swayed. She rocked in an unseen tide and her vision blurred. With a breath, her training engaged and the door within her poured open. Rushing waters cascaded around her, pulling at her consciousness. Exhaling slowly, she closed her eyes and spilled with the waters into the Otherworld.

A river carries her. Swift and clear, the waters run between deep, earthen banks. Coursing with the tide, Bree's awareness rushes. Freed of form, at one with the waters, she flows. As her soul sluices and churns bank and riverbed, her consciousness spans the river and she realizes—she is alone.

"Allies be with me." Her call ripples the waters.

A gentle presence enfolds her. Steady and fatherly, it whispers reassurance. "Trust. You are safe. I will carry you to her."

A song washes through Bree. Peaceful and soothing, it sings an undulating promise of Love. Exhaling deeper into the waters, she drifts in its tender murmur.

"Come, Raven Child."

Bree smiles. She knows that voice. "Mother Gaia."

A hand hovers before her. Drawing up her awareness, Bree reaches outward and reclaims human skin. Her outstretched hand makes contact and a motherly touch enfolds her own. White light flashes. Bree closes her eyes against the brilliance and the cool comfort of the waters recedes.

Opening her eyes, Bree finds herself standing. Fully human once more, her feet rest bare upon soft, green earth. Before her, a beautiful laurel tree rises out of that earth and basks in spilling sunshine. Bree drops her gaze and sends it travelling up the tree. Nine broad roots emerge out of the dark, loamy soil and curve upward to birth a thick trunk covered in grey bark. Graceful branches stretch outward, lifting countless grey-green leaves into the streaming sunlight. Bree inhales sharply. For a moment, ghostly arms hover within the branches.

"What is this place?" she wonders aloud.

"This is the answer your client seeks."

Bree shifts her gaze toward the resonant voice. Mother Gaia stands to her left, brilliant green eyes watching her.

The earth goddess gestures toward the laurel tree. "This is Daphne."

Bree considers the radiant tree. This is Daphne O'Shea?

The branches of the tree shimmer and sway. Bree turns her head but no wind rustles her hair or cloak. As her gaze falls again upon the dancing limbs, the bark shivers and a being, gossamer white, steps out of the trunk.

"You misunderstand, Raven Child," the Tree Spirit walks toward her. "I am not your client. I am Daphne."

Bree frowns and glances over her left shoulder. Peering through the Veil, she can see her client, still sitting on the lavender floor cushion in the den of Bree's thatched cottage in Kildare. The white light of Brighid's loving shelter enfolds her like a halo.

"Hunted." The Otherworldly word aches through Bree, echoing until it dissolves into her client's voice. "My relationships always end badly," the woman laments. "What is wrong with me? Why must I always run away from love?"

"My client is named Daphne." Bree faces the Tree Spirit. "Daphne O'Shea."

"Quite fitting," Mother Gaia nods.

"She is aptly named..." The Tree Spirit places her hand upon her heart. "...After me." Blue eyes gleam through the dappling light. "She runs because she knows—" Daphne gestures toward her laurel tree.

"Love will change her."

"Love always changes you." Mother Gaia's voice washes over Bree as she observes Daphne's tree. "Love rebirths you into a new form. If it is True Love, it sets you free and restores your Truest form."

"You see," Daphne's gaze catches and locks with Bree's. "I was not always a tree. I was born of the river."

The fatherly touch of the waters washes through Bree and her eyes widen. "Peneus…" She exhales the words as a whisper.

Daphne and Mother Gaia nod.

Awe spills through Bree and she bows. Daphne, the Greek Naiad, she marvels silently. Daphne, the beloved of Apollo. Daphne who, running from love, became the laurel tree. "Peace be upon you, Lady."

Rising from her bow, Bree finds herself bathed in the glinting blue of Daphne's eyes.

"He was true to me, in his own way."

"Apollo?"

The former Naiad nods. Walking closer to her tree, she runs her fingers through her leaves. "In the end, he honored me, made my leaves into a crown of excellence." She stands staring at her trunk, then reaches to touch a well-worn spot in the grey bark. "He used to come and sit with me. He would tell me his dreams, whisper his hopes to me. Nights he would spend nestled at my feet, sharing all the details of his day."

Letting her hand fall back to her side, she lifts her gaze toward the sun lowering overhead. "Had he wooed me thus, it might have been different. We might have had a chance." She drops her gaze and faces Bree. Daphne's blue eyes churn dark and stormy. "Instead, he chased me. He forced me to run."

Daphne shakes her head. "I wanted only the Wild. I thrived with the hunt, until I became the hunted.

Then, all that mattered was my freedom." She lifts her gaze back to the lowering sun. "But it might have been different, had he honored my Wildness and shown me his own tenderly."

Mother Gaia sighs. Bree turns her head toward the goddess and voices rush past her. Daphne's voice. Mother Gaia's. Snippets of endless debates stream through her and Bree wonders if this is an old conversation.

Daphne looks at Mother Gaia and offers the earth goddess a wan smile. "Can a river truly love the Sun and be loved by the Sun in full freedom?"

The image of a stream glistening in the sunlight fills Bree's awareness. She sees the river, bathed endlessly in the loving sun. Day after day, the heat of that lover's touch caresses the waters and night after night, the river runs smaller and more shallow than the day before. Slowly the river shrinks, until it disappears completely—evaporated, consumed in the touch of its lover. Its light extinguished, only darkness remains.

Light spills through the darkness, like sunlight dappling through leaves. Bree blinks and Daphne stands before her. The Naiad, now Tree Spirit, runs her eyes up the trunk of her own tree and along her branches.

"Perhaps we had a better chance this way."

Bree considers the laurel tree before her. She can see the sunlight spilling down to kiss its limbs, the grey-green leaves drinking in that loving radiance. A gentle humming washes through her as the tree quivers with the joy of photosynthesis.

"Certainly a tree can drink the Love of the Sun more freely," Mother Gaia murmurs.

Daphne nods slowly, then looks at Bree. The blue eyes glisten with unshed tears. "Perhaps I was too young to see Love, to hear its thrum of Wildness. Perhaps if he had let me see himself, see the Love that he is, that he offers. If he had honored my Wildness, met Wildness with Wildness..." She sighs and runs her fingertips down the bark of her tree. "But, then I would never have stood at one with the Wild. I would *never have felt the robins nesting in my arms, or heard the first cries of newborn chicks. I would never have known the relief and gratitude of the owl, hovering in shelter from the storm. Nor witnessed the delight and joy of bear cubs at play.*"

She lifts her face again to the Sun. "*I would never have understood—All things need Love to thrive.*"

"*Is this what you would tell Daphne, my client? Lady, is this your answer to her?*" Bree watches the Tree Spirit gaze tenderly at the Sun. Tears spill slowly down Daphne's cheeks. Then Daphne lowers her gaze to Bree.

"*And this. Any hunt promises only to destroy its participants. For only Death—not Love—comes with the hunt and claims its bounty in the running.*" Daphne shakes her head. "*She must give it up. If she is ever to truly know Love, she must give up the hunt.*"

The Tree Spirit drops her gaze to the ground. Sighing softly, she walks toward the trunk and stands with her feet nestled upon two roots. Bree draws breath to speak, but hesitates. Daphne rests her head against the bark of her tree, then turns suddenly.

She casts blazing eyes upon Bree. "*It is true— Love will change her. But she must welcome that change. She must let Love woo her, let Wildness honor Wildness. Only then will Love set her free.*"

Daphne steps backward. The Tree Spirit's toes touch the bark of the laurel tree. Shimmering gossamer white, they sink into the trunk, followed by one radiant leg, then the other. As Daphne's torso disappears into the trunk of her tree, Bree steps forward.

"*How? How may Daphne, my client, give up the hunt and choose to woo and be wooed? How may she embrace Love?*"

Daphne's face hovers just below the bark of the tree. Pieces appear to rise and fall as she replies. "*She must remember this always—All things need Love to thrive. All beings are Love embodied and all Love deserves to thrive."

The bark snaps into stillness as the face dissolves into the trunk. Bree looks up as the branches sway, but no breeze disturbs her hair. The grey-green leaves rustle above her and, for a moment, she can see long, thin fingers stretching just below the skin of the branches.

Bree walks up and kisses the bark of the tree. "Thank you, Lady," she whispers. "Blessed is the Mystery."

Placing her bare feet carefully to avoid stepping on the roots of the laurel tree, Bree takes three steps backwards, then turns. Mother Gaia raises open arms to her.

"Come, Raven Child," the earth goddess smiles.

Bree approaches and places her hands into those of Mother Gaia.

"Come, he would speak with you."

Tender warmth enfolds Bree's right hand as the earth goddess wraps Bree's hand in Her own. Together they walk, hand in hand, toward the river. As they draw near, the waters churn and spill upward into the flowing form of a man.

"Peneus..." Bree exhales.

The water spirit, father of Daphne, places a streaming hand over his heart and bows. "Peace be upon you, Raven Child."

"Peace be between us," Bree replies, offering a bow of her own.

Rising to stand face to face again, they finish the ritual greeting together. "Now and through all time."

Bree smiles. "Do you have a message for my client?"

"And for you."

"For me?" Surprise ripples her voice.

Peneus nods. "What father would not be proud to see his child the beloved of a god?

Yet, I knew—Daphne enjoyed the hunt too much. She could not allow Love to reshape her. Your Daphne is the same. So, Raven Child, are you.

"Welcome the reshaping and allow Love to reveal to you who you truly are. Let your Wildness be *your strength and hold you centered in your soul. But let the Wildness of another meet your own—peacefully, honestly, tenderly. Then where the two touch, the nurturing milk of Love will flow."*

Peneus smiles. "Love blossoms only between equals, between those who choose to thrive and wish for their lover to thrive as well."

"I don't trust people enough to allow them to woo me."

A tear slipped down her client's cheek and Bree nodded. "As Daphne said, you must give that up."

Blue eyes flashed from the shadows obscuring her client's face. "What if I can't? What if I don't want to?"

Waves of fear rolled off the woman before Bree, buffeting her awareness. Bree exhaled. "Do you want to know Love in this lifetime?"

The woman's chin quivered, then dipped.

"Then you must approach Love and loving differently." Bree lowered her gaze and leaned slightly forward on her cushion. Her eyes searched amongst the shadows for those of her client. Blue sparked before her, then vanished.

"How?"

"Allow Love to approach you peacefully." Bree watched the dappling light drift across the woman seated on the lavender floor cushion opposite her. "Instead of hunting out what you desire in another and pursuing it ruthlessly, seek it first within yourself. Cultivate your own unique beauty and learn to live in it. Learn to love it, to nourish it, to want it to thrive.

Then, see the beauty others cultivate within themselves. Celebrate that beauty. Call Love to you by encouraging the beauty of others and of yourself to grow equally."

The candle flame sputtered on the altar and Bree paused. Flickering harshly, it sent wisps of dark smoke billowing skyward. As the flame dimmed once more, Bree called silently to her Otherworldly Teacher. *Goddess Bríghid, help her, please.*

Blue eyes blazed before Bree as Daphne O'Shea exhaled. The candle flame shuddered, then steadied. Bree sat in silence, waiting, her eyes fixed on the shrunken flame. Slowly, it stretched upward. When it gleamed again in full brightness, Bree lifted her gaze to meet Daphne's.

"When you find someone who can do this with you, equally and peacefully, you will know Love."

◆　◆　◆

Bree strolled along the slowly curving lane, her square-toed boots pressing gently into the moist, Kildare earth. As a breeze caught and pulled at the edges of her black hair, she lifted her gaze and smiled. Lowering overhead, the sun spilled golden-red on its journey westward.

Peaceful night, Apollo.

Bree's stride shortened until she stood staring at the fading light. Red stretched into the darkening sky like branches and an image of Daphne's laurel tree flooded her inner vision. Shimmering before her, familiar gossamer white fingers caressed a well-worn spot in the grey bark of the trunk.

"*He used to come and sit with me. He would tell me his dreams, whisper his hopes to me. Nights he would spend nestled at my feet, sharing all the details of his day.*" Daphne's voice echoed through her. "*Had he wooed me thus, it might have been different. We might have had a chance.*"

Cool air rustled her hair and Bree

shivered. The grey bark of her vision wavered and dissolved into the setting sun.

"She'll be waiting for you," Bree breathed into the twilight.

A solitary golden beam lanced through the growing darkness, then was gone. Bree smiled and pressed her hand to her heart.

"Blessed is the Mystery."

Her breath hovered on the air and Bree pulled her favorite black fleece jacket more tightly around her. Still shivering in the growing cold, she stooped to zip it closed. A gentle warmth spilled up her legs and wrapped her in its Otherworldly blanket. As she straightened, brilliant green eyes caught her.

She inhaled sharply. "Mother Gaia."

"Hello, Raven Child."

Bree bowed her head to the earth goddess, then returned the emerald gaze. "I am surprised to meet you here," Bree gestured to the earth around her, "on Éire's Isle."

Mother Gaia laughed softly. *"I knew Eirene, and her two sisters, long before the Olympians drove her out of Greece."* The goddess tilted her head. *"You could say we are old friends."*

"Is that what brings you here tonight? An old friend?"

"It is," Mother Gaia smiled. *"But not Eirene."*

Bree shook her head. "I don't understand."

"I know."

Mother Gaia lifted her gaze and stared into the sky. Following the goddess' gaze, Bree watched a small patch of scarlet draining into darkness.

"If Apollo had been more like Fergus, perhaps he would have won Daphne."

"Fergus?" Bree turned startled eyes to the earth goddess. "What does Fergus Sinclair have to do with this?"

Still staring into the deepening night, Mother Gaia

smiled.

Hazel eyes sparkled in her awareness as the deep, resonant laugh of her friend rumbled through Bree. Exhaling softly, she closed her eyes to the darkening Kildare night and fiery red hair flamed into view.

"*C'mon MacLeod,*" Fergus' voice drifted from memory, "*Time for some food.*" As the vision flooded, Bree watched a younger, nearly exhausted version of herself look up from the pile of medical books she had been hunched over for days. Lost in her studies for the upcoming board exams, Bree had forgotten to eat. Fergus had brought her coffee and a much needed home-cooked meal.

Crimson light flooded and receded to reveal a pair of Cardinal's baseball tickets. The words "Opening Day" stretched in looping, white letters across the stubs. He had purchased the tickets as a gift, part of his master plan to educate her about his city. Bree watched herself look up at Fergus's smiling face. "*You said you wanted to see Saint Louis at its best.*"

The sparkling sunlight behind Fergus faded to night. Despite the cool, evening air, they were seated outside on the patio of Café de Lys. "*So,*" his face fell serious as he raised his porcelain coffee mug, "*what do I say? Happy Samhain?*" Bree heard herself laugh gently and reply, "Blessed Samhain." How many hours had they sat in those chairs discussing the nature of life, death and the Mystery? They had met through a colleague, another practitioner of the healing arts, but the Café was where their friendship truly began.

Gwen's Café.

Bree opened her eyes.

Fergus had been there for her then, too. He came to the hospital just to drive Bree home. He even stayed with her that night, rocking her on the couch and listening to her repeat over and over, "DOA."

"*He loves you.*" Gwen's voice echoed from the Otherworld into the Kildare night. "*Trust in Love again.*"

Tears welled in Bree's eyes, blurring her vision. She was so tired of crying. She had marked the past year with weeping—every fire festival, each turning of the moon. Still, sorrow hunted her. Staring into the darkness, she shivered and let her tears fall.

Warmth enveloped Bree as Mother Gaia enfolded her in loving arms. "*All things need Love to thrive, Raven Child, including you.*"

For more, visit: ThroughShamansEyes.wordpress.com

61 Angelica Street

Lynn Obermoeller

From 1933 to 1963, Mississippi Valley Stockyards at 61 Angelica Street was the last stop for cows, horses, pigs and sheep before they were slaughtered. Most animals ended up at Krey Packing, also in St. Louis, or shipped out to other meat manufacturers.

My husband's Grandpa Harry worked in the hog yard. He took the hogs off the trucks, fed them to fatten them up, weighed them, and then loaded the pigs back on the truck to get slaughtered. Grandpa Harry used a cane that he'd smack on the ground or sometimes he'd whack the back of a pig, and yell, "Sue-ee, sue-ee, pig, pig, pig, sue-ee," as he'd move the hogs up and down the alley.

At the age of 16, Harry's son Norman started working at Mississippi Valley Stockyards, and eventually he became the Weigh Master for the cattle and overall foreman. He sat on a bench inside a cage that had a glass wall in front of him. Norman would zero the old fashioned scale with weights before the cows entered. One worker would manually open the gate to let the cows into a pen, which was the scale. Once the cows were in the pen, the weight was determined. Norman wrote on a card the owner's name, the number of cows the owner brought in and their weight. After he finished, he'd ring a bell that signaled workers to open the other gate and let the cows out.

Norman often worked the night shift at Mississippi Valley. He'd bring his wife, Maurine, and their boys, Norm Jr. (my husband) and Dale, to keep him company in between rounds. The boys slept on the wooden bench outside, listening to whistling trains rumble down the tracks that divided the 81 acres between Broadway and the Mississippi River. Meanwhile, Norman walked through the entire complex doing his nightly rounds. He inserted a special key into a series of red boxes. When the key was twisted, it sounded a signal to the police. Each red box was called a "point." After point one, Norman had a certain amount of time to get to point two and turn that key. If he didn't sound the alarm in the given time, it was a signal something was wrong at the stockyard.

Back in those days cattle rustlers would attempt to steal cattle. Rustlers would come to the back of the stockyards with their lights off on their truck, grab a cow or pig, load it in the back and drive away. Stealing didn't happen a lot, but if Norman was on duty and a rustler was trying to steal a cow, Norman wouldn't have time to insert the key, alarming the police.

When the boys got older, they'd accompany their dad when he made his rounds. As he'd insert the keys at the various points, he'd turn on the alley lights. The light caused all the rats to freeze in place. Norm Jr. and Dale fired off rounds from a .22 single-shot rifle and killed as many rats as they could. The first shot let out a bang, startling all the other rats to run. After there were no more rats scurrying around, the boys would fire hose the dead rats, along with all the manure, into the open sewers.

Upon arrival, it took the boys about 15 minutes before they got used to the overpowering barnyard smell. It was so strong they could see the fumes rising from the manure, especially in the summer. The stench rivaled the smell of the hops from the nearby brewery. Norm Jr. and Dale always knew when their dad walked into the house... he smelled just like the stockyards.

The foul odor didn't stop folks like Handsome Hambone Haggerty from eating at the stockyard restaurant, "Hoof & Horn." It also didn't stop Norm Jr. and Dale from building forts and tunnels out of the bales of hay. Nothing stopped the boys from having fun. When it was time to go fishing, they'd take a pitchfork, turn over the manure and find the biggest worms ever.

The possibility of fun was around every corner, but trouble wasn't too far, either. One time a bull got loose; it tore up four police cars before it ended up on Grand Avenue. The bull stood in front of a shop window where it collapsed and died from exhaustion.

Another time, Buck Jr. - just an eight-year-old boy way beyond his years - picked up the testicles of a newly castrated bull with a stick. He twirled the testicles around as if he was lassoing a calf. The testicles flung off the stick and landed right on top of his dad's brand new Stetson cowboy hat. Old man Buck was none too happy and little Buck paid dearly.

Norm Jr. and Dale were thrilled when Miss Elliott, a breeder who boarded some of her horses at the stockyards—the same horses that raced at Cahokia Downs and Fairmont Park Race Track—allowed the boys to ride the horses.

Norm Jr. nicknamed the owner and president of the stockyard, Carroll P. Poland, "Truman" after the U.S. President. Dale, however, called him "Hitler" because he felt Poland was always calling his dad into the office and chewing him out for something.

In 1963, Mississippi Valley Stockyards closed its doors forever. Grandpa Harry retired. Norman, after 25 years at the stockyards, was fortunate to find another job in St. Louis, MO.

Although little history is available on this by-gone era, my husband and his brother have fond memories growing up in the city of St. Louis, yet experiencing farm life at 61 Angelica Street.

Bellefontaine Cemetery

Steven Langhorst

One hundred thousand daffodils bloom along paths
covering forgotten streams and stories

Marking the edges of plots that hold spent flowers
planted long ago.

The HEMPSTEADS grew in the far corner until one by
one

Each one was planted in the earth.

Beneath the shade of the champion shingle oak are
markers for the gardens of

PRUFROCK, SIMPSON, PITCAIRN and DURHAM. Each
one faded and silent.

Follow the shining blossoms to find warriors, explorers,
engineers, brewers, bankers, the old and YOUNG, poets
and pilots.

GUERRIN, VON der AHE, TEASDALE, EDWARDS,

Each planting holds a story of lives and loves
and loss.

BURROUGHS, SHREVE, EADS,

CHIPMAN, and CLARK.

Stories in stone of adventure and heroes, exploring and inventing.

Walk along the flowers to find MOTHER next to FATHER, and BABY alone.

DR. AUGUST lies next to his beloved ornament, AUGUSTA.

And the men who built towns are scattered around.

One marker is named STONE, another is LAMB.

Shrouded Angels and Urns mark where the stories turned.

Wild flowers carpet the plots of MASONS and CHILDREN of EDGEWOOD.

FLORAL was a cherished wife and SARAH and SARA are planted close to one another.

FRANCIS is next to FRANCES and LEWIS shadows LOUIS among names too worn to call.

Follow each daffodil and greet eighty-seven thousand blooms buried.

In Bellefontaine some flowers are buried then bloom and some bloom and then are buried.

Stop at any one to listen to the story and

The once bloomed and planted bloom once more.

The Most Haunted Prison in America

Shelly X. Leonn

Something about the morning sun always made Vernon feel reflective. He leaned back on his palms and turned his face to the sky. "Well." He blew some smoke from his mouth as his eyes traced the horizon, washed in the pinks and yellows of a deceptively peaceful dawn. "At least it's a nice morning."

"Yeah." Cleo smiled at her hands, which she kept folded in her lap. Vernon wondered if she buried them to conceal their trembling. "Yeah, it is."

Underneath them, the Missouri River flowed and churned, impassive in its endless journey to convergence with the Mississippi.

A few hours earlier, Vernon and Cleo had strolled along the pedestrian walkway of the Jefferson City Bridge. An endless parade of vehicles passed them by, heading into the city. Among the throng, Vernon had spotted local news trucks as well as a few big names in national news.

Cleo had suggested they go back, maybe try to ruffle the reporters' feathers a bit for the cameras.

But both of them knew the suggestion was as empty as the prison itself. They couldn't return. Not now, not ever.

Without words, they resolved to sit over the edge of the bridge. Their bodies phased through the guardrails and their legs dangled above the swift river as they watched the sunrise.

"It's a pretty city, too," Cleo observed.

Vernon nodded. "Mmm," he muttered in agreement. From the bridge, they could see the outline of the state capitol building. Its white dome's silhouette appeared black as the first rays of sunshine touched it. "Were you here, when they finished that?"

"Yes." Cleo sneered, a slight upturning of her full lips. "They brought in an architect from New York. Like we need a Yankee designing our state's center."

Vernon chuckled. "You really are a Midwest girl, aren't you?"

"Always have been, always will be," she replied, then paused. Vernon knew the reason for her hesitation. What had once been a matter of "always will be" had, in one night, been taken from them. Their bleak, new reality pressed upon them, shifting the tone and topic of conversation. Cleo swallowed, then asked, "Have you heard from Moira?"

"No." Vernon took another thoughtful pull from his cigarette.

"What about Juliana?"

"No."

The trembles of panic caused her voice to waver. "Nathaniel?"

"I haven't heard from anyone, Cleo." Vernon felt strangely detached from the entire conversation as if he had always known this moment lurked around the bend. Even his own replies felt rehearsed, maybe even predestined. "I think they're already gone."

"That can't be true." Cleo sniffed, her slim nose flaring as she drew in air. "They wouldn't just leave us. They wouldn't give up."

Her declaration snapped him into the moment. "What choice did they have?" Vernon shot back with heat in his tone. "Don't blame them, Cleo. They did what made sense. Maybe we should have done the same."

Cleo's features flickered. "You don't mean that?"

After taking a final drag, Vernon sent his cigarette over the side of the bridge. It turned in circles and arcs as it approached the water, glinting with the golden rays of the sunrise. Before it hit the water, it disappeared in a puff of ethereal essence. As he pondered the possible answers to her question, his own conviction grew. "I do." He stared at her, his gaze even and unwavering.

A moment passed. Cleo's eyes, clouded mirrors of the radiating blue orbs he remembered from her life, pleaded with him without words.

But Vernon maintained his steady stare.

With a sigh of surrender, Cleo dropped her head into her hands.

Both of them knew the truth. Their time had run out. They had to leave.

I'm ready to go, he thought. At last, he released that thought, a thought he had kept locked deep within himself for decades—no, centuries. It felt like releasing a captured insect from his cupped hands.

And once he gave it flight, he couldn't call it back.

Vernon sensed his presence before he saw him. He gave off a weighted, grave atmosphere, as heavy as a granite stone sinking into the impassive river flowing under the bridge.

"You summoned me?" he asked, his voice like teeth grinding gravel.

Vernon shrugged. "I guess so."

Cleo sniffled, then cried in earnest. "I don't want to leave." She sounded like a sniveling child, mewling into her mother's skirts.

"Mrs. Brandon, please don't make a fuss about this." To Vernon's surprise, the looming presence approached them, then sat on Vernon's right side, his own legs garbed in cheerless black also dangling over the water. But he kept a tight grip on his curved scythe, letting Vernon know the old god never let his guard down, not completely.

He let out a sigh and wiped his brow,

invisible in the deep cowl of his hood. "It's been a long night, you see."

"I thought you'd be dancing a jig when you caught up to us," Cleo snipped back as she blew her nose on her sleeve. "How many years have you been after us?"

He clucked his tongue with annoyance, then chucked a rock over the side of the bridge with a flick of his long, bony fingers. "Only doing my job, madam. And, even you must admit, you and your friends have defied the rules of unlife for a very, very long time."

"Yeah," Vernon agreed. "Yeah, we have."

"I'm not without feeling." He quieted his voice until it barely breached the volume of a whisper. "Nights like tonight are hard on everyone." He gave Vernon a consoling pat on his leg. "I did enjoy our games of cat and mouse, old friends. And no one, not even me, wanted the game to end like this."

Cleo didn't seem to hear him. With the last of her pride, she stammered, "I am Cleo the Cleaver! I murdered twenty women with my butcher knife! I made a paranormal investigator faint with a touch on the shoulder."

Vernon knew half of that story was hyperbole and the other half complete fabrication, but he knew better than to press the issue with a woman on the brink of a meltdown. Besides, he couldn't act superior. After all, Vernon the Cannibal had his own tall tales that he maintained to keep the guests coming back.

Biting her lip, Cleo sputtered out, "I've—I've been on The Discovery Channel for my appearances in the hospital ward in my blood-stained dress!" She slammed her tight fist into the ground. "I will not be beaten by some—by some …"

"Act of God?" Vernon finished for her, but he also directed the question at the grim figure seated next to him.

"You're asking me?" he asked, pressing a fleshless hand to his breast. "If a God exists, I have yet to make its acquaintance. I have a job to do, and I do it. And nights like last night ..." He trailed off, as if replaying the destruction and chaos he must have spent all night navigating through his eternal mind.

Even though Vernon couldn't see his eyes, the slight shift in his cowl suggested he, too, gazed at the city's skyline as he pondered. "Not even I know why these things happen. Why one house is left untouched, and another demolished, killing the mother, father, little children, and pets inside. Or—" He directed his black face in their direction, pressing all the weight of his eternal existence and duty upon them. "—why prisons like Missouri State Penitentiary allow ghosts like you two to cheat me for more days than I care to count."

"The most haunted prison in America, reduced to rubble!" Cleo cried, then fell into Vernon's waiting arms. He clung to her, smoothing her hair and shushing her, as she mumbled more words into his chest. "Nothing scares us. Nothing!"

"I have to admit, I was impressed when I heard you two tried to flee." The figure stood, brushing off his black robes. "Everyone else asked me to take them at that moment. But you two? You had to make it theatrical, didn't you?"

Vernon also rose, helping Cleo to her feet as he did so. "Well, would you expect anything less from Vernon the Cannibal and Cleo the Clever?"

He chuckled. "No, I suppose not." With a gesture of his scythe, the old god directed their attention to the morning sun, which was moments from complete sunrise. "And you can't maintain your existence here when day arrives, anyway. Seems a little pointless for you to call me."

"Just do it, old friend. For old time's sake."

The figure nodded. Vernon imagined his hidden face smirking. Then, he leveled his scythe at them.

Vernon and Cleo ceased to be.

With honor, love, and respect to

everyone *and everything affected by the Jefferson City tornado on May 23, 2019.*

The Missouri State Penitentiary was damaged but not destroyed and was scheduled to reopen in October.

To Build a Better Coffin

Fedora Amis

Foreword

In the days before doctors could firmly draw the line between life and death, many people feared being buried alive. In 1852 George Bateson patented his "Life Revival Device," commonly known as "Bateson's Belfry." George built a contraption with a bell at the top of a shaft reaching down into a coffin. Through the shaft ran a rope from the bell to the hands of the possibly un-dead for the un-corpse to ring for rescue. Queen Victoria was so impressed that she bestowed upon him the Order of the British Empire in 1859, an action she may have later regretted. Bateson became so obsessed with premature entombment that he took radical measures to insure himself against such a hideous fate. He gave rise to the expression "Bats in the belfry" when he poured linseed oil over his body and set himself on fire--so the myth goes. The story isn't true, yet I dedicate the following to all dreamers who have sought...

St. Louis, Missouri
1871

Few activities invigorate mind and body so agreeably as a brisk trot to the cemetery on a crisp March night. Short legs a-churn, Inglefuss Muckenecker bubbled with impatience as he pumped his way past crews scooping up horse manure from the dirt streets of St. Louis.

A balding little man with a body even thinner than his hair, "Old Twice-as-Fussy" as his employees called him when his back was turned, never felt happier than when he could accomplish two things at once. To wit, he distracted the eye from his scanty wisps of hair and proved he was a true Republican by wearing a full set of bushy whiskers.

As Ingle trotted through the gates of Bellefontaine Cemetery, he spied lanterns and a clutch of men around a mound of dirt. One grunted from the effort of prying open a casket with a crowbar.

Ingle's heart thumped in his ear when a digger tucked his nose into the crook of his arm and leaned on his spade. Bad sign, that.

Fearing the worst, Ingle came to a wobbly halt at grave's edge. The doctor who had summoned him raised a white-gloved hand to keep Ingle back. "Sorry, Mr. Muckenecker. You don't want to look."

"I haven't come all this way in the middle of the night to turn coward at sight of the grim reaper's scythe. A person in my profession sees a good deal of his handiwork."

The doctor pulled down a white silk shroud from the bloated head of a female cadaver. "I warned you this could happen. Gases from putrefaction caused the body to swell. That's what pulled down her hands and rang the bell."

Ingle blinked back tears--not from seeing his mother in such a state, but because Bateson's Belfry Coffin had failed. For two years he had schemed to get his hands on the plans. Two years wasted.

His dreams of inventing the world's best coffin melted and began running out his nose. He snuffed them back. Ingle had banked his future on becoming coffinmaker to the American West. He had already optioned a warehouse to hold the splendid output from the factory he had yet to build.

Dismay set in. His life's fulfillment demanded that he manufacture countless repositories so that the newly rich could spend eternity in comfort. What's more, in a "Genuine Muckenecker" patrons could go to their final reward with serene hearts. Should their interment have been too hasty, Muckenecker guaranteed a speedy return to the land of bratwurst and beer.

The doctor spat a stream of tobacco juice into the hole in the ground. "You should have embalmed her. One good thing to come out of the War Between the States was arsenic embalming fluid. Never bloat then. Used arsenic on Lincoln himself. Mark my words. Someday embalming will become common as Winkelmeyer beer at Winkelmeyer's saloon."

The doctor issued orders to the diggers. "Seal 'er up and put 'er down." He departed with a pat on Ingle's shoulder. "I wish you had taken my advice."

As they tipped hats to each other in the shadowy moonlight, Ingle stood straight as a poker. "Don't apologize. I needed to see for myself."

Plodding home, Ingle considered what to do. The doctor says embalming is the way of the future. If he's right, nobody will want a coffin designed to save people from premature burial. No big factory. No millionaire's wealth.

He might not even be able to afford his fine new townhouse. He envisioned telling his wife he could no longer lavish her with the niceties of carriage and driver, maid, laundress. He shuddered to think what that would mean.

His wife was a big woman, easily twice his weight and a foot taller as well. Ingle blinked back tears, not from fearing his wife's wrath, but because he had failed her. He didn't feel love for the giantess he had married-- not love. Pride that he could master so imposing a creature.

That was the heart of his problem. He prized Olga and needed most desperately to earn her--not love.

Respect. He had gained her esteem by making money to buy her the social position she coveted. Placing her in the upper echelons of St. Louis society, as she deserved, took heavy pockets.

Ingle's greatest pleasure was his marriage. The fact that his Olga was well-dowered as well as well-endowed further increased his satisfaction. The thought of his wife dressed in hoopskirts so wide no one could come within eight feet of her created a stir in his loins. Well, that decided things. He had to succeed.

He refused to be crushed by competition and criticism as his father had been. If Ingle could build a better coffin, he would push Olga to the pinnacle of society while simultaneously vindicating his father's faith in coffins. Enchanted by the twin prospects, he rubbed his hands in excitement--and warmed them at the same time.

He resolved to redouble his efforts. He might yet win big at the coffin-construction game. He would provide something everyone needed--a bulwark against death. Or at least a small bulkhead against being buried alive.

As for embalming, ridiculous. Who but the insane would choose arsenic water over blood as the proper fluid in the veins of a deceased beloved?

Deep in his soul, he knew families did not always look upon their dearly departed with tender feelings. He had been asked on several occasions to build coffins with hidden vials of cyanide or chlorine gas in the coffin rim. When workmen fitted the lid and drove home the nails, the vials would break and spew poison over the body--thus banishing any chance the corpse would make an inconvenient resurrection. Ingle, honorable man that he was, had never complied. He knew others did.

So what if some people preferred dead relatives' money over dead relatives? Many people bought coffins for themselves. They yearned for life and would snap up the anti-death assurance a Genuine Muckenecker offered.

He took heart. The hour was only a little past midnight when he aimed himself toward his place of business. By sunup when the shop foreman arrived, Ingle had nearly finished plans for "Muckenecker's Majestic Memorial Coffin." His six grand improvements would make him the brightest star in the coffin-making heavens.

Bleary-eyed, he handed the plans to the foreman. "Build it."

While Ingle slipped into his frock coat and prepared to go home for much needed sleep, the foreman pored over the plans. "I don't see the size specifications."

"Must I do everything? Build it big enough to put in all the innovations. And have it done this afternoon."

The foreman's head shot up in disbelief. "The most we can do is nail and sand."

"Well, of course it is. I don't expect shellac and silk lining." Thoroughly out of sorts, Ingle barked, "Just make the box. Caulk it so it's waterproof and air-tight. You can do that, can't you?"

Back home, he would have gone straight to bed but for his wife's insistence on food. Olga hustled up a light breakfast of toast with jam, ham, sausages, grits, bacon, potatoes, scrapple, eggs, cinnamony streusel coffeecake and boiled carrots. He ate dutifully but refused both coffee and tea.

He slept until past noon, then hurried to his shop without eating a midday meal despite Olga's pleas that he was already too thin. He felt no hunger for anything but his masterpiece.

To his cheerful distress, he found his business had been swamped with orders for cheap plank caskets. "What's this, a new outbreak of cholera?"

Ingle was half-appalled, half-eager. Cholera had set the cornerstone for his success. He had built coffins as the final place of residence for a goodly number of the 3527 locals who died of cholera in the 1866 epidemic. That lucrative source of business had all but dried up on account of a healthy influx of cash into the St. Louis sewer system. In 1867 the city chalked up a paltry 684 deaths to the dread disease, which could turn a pink-cheeked youth into a gray corpse in a single day.

Ingle could find little cause for optimism in other diseases. Yellow fever seldom traveled as far north as Missouri. Thanks to quinine, malaria had not been fatal since Dr. Sappington led the way. After the big war, doctors routinely doused patients with Q at the first sign of fever.

Smallpox vaccinations worked when people chose science over superstition. Of course, one could hope for outbreaks of influenza or war, but those were far too undependable.

He would have to make his fortune from the day-to-day death toll of childbirth, accident, pneumonia, suicide and good old reliable "Natural Causes." The only way to persuade folks to buy his products instead of cheaper ones--or, heaven forbid, be embalmed--was to build a better coffin.

He yelled at the foreman over the din of hammering. "Are you deaf? I asked what happened."

The foreman cupped his hands to magnify his words, "Riverboat explosion. Owner of the line ordered pine boxes to ship home the dead. He wanted the bodies nailed in as soon as might be. Catfish been at some of them."

Ingle looked around in confusion. "What about my coffin? Have you done nothing I expressly ordered you to do?"

With a perplexed look on his ruddy face, the foreman motioned toward a three-foot-deep, seven foot by seven foot wooden box leaning against the wall.

Ingle frowned as he pointed. "That's for a piano, not a person."

"You didn't say how big to make it so I added half-a-foot for each of them improvements."

"What's wrong with you, man? This monstrosity

would need two four-foot wide burial plots."

"Easy enough to cut the bracing and take it apart."

"No, you have your hands full. As usual, I have to do everything myself."

His next problem was where to put the consarned thing. Every inch of space inside his shop, including his own office, had been commandeered.

Only one option came to mind. Take the big box home. He sent a boy to fetch drayage men as he set about piling up stocks of nails, canvas and glue. He left a message for the haulers to meet him at the Turnverein Hall after loading. At the Turner Hall, he expected to locate some very special goods he needed for his project.

When his wife saw the huge box, she was more than a little perturbed. "Box too big. It fit novhere but front parlor. Vould ruin carpet from Turkey."

"Men, roll up the carpet before you set up the sawhorses. Cover the furniture, Olga. The box is going in the parlor."

"Vhat about new brocade drapes?"

"Cover them too."

"Cover drapes? Not can be done."

"Then take them down."

"Neighbors vould stare."

"Might be good advertising. Muckenecker--a man who works long into the night to build a better coffin."

Olga raced about to cover furniture with sheets while the maid took down the drapery. Ingle had not thought to bring sawhorses from the shop. Of course, the shop could ill-spare them if he had. He fetched his own pair from the cellar, but they turned out to be woefully inadequate.

The parlor simply was not big enough to lay both box and heavy coffin lid on the floor. He had to work on the lid, so the body of the box had to rest precariously on sawhorses. The box teetered when weight was applied to any corner. Even so, Ingle had to risk it.

While Ingle set to work, Olga flounced off in a snit to dis-invite ladies she had asked to tea.

He reasoned thus: To survive when waking in a grave, a person must accomplish the following in order: signal, breathe, eat, drink, excrete and pass the time pleasantly and productively.

Goals established, Ingle set about building the prototype for Muckenecker's Majestic.

First Goal: Signal the outside world. He drilled a hole in the coffin lid and fitted in an eight-foot length of pipe. Through the pipe, he ran rope attached to a bell at the top and a policeman's whistle at the bottom.

To magnify sound he drilled the side of a brass megaphone and scooted it down over the above-grave end of the pipe. The blow horn had a happy secondary purpose. It would keep rainwater from gushing in. Wouldn't want a fellow to drown in his own coffin.

Ingle was hard at work on his second goal by the time Olga returned home. Still in a huff, she tromped to the kitchen without a word.

To allow for physical necessity, he nailed a shallow basin on a knob which could move up and down a greased track to accommodate a person of any height. All the undertaker needed to do was slide in the fanny of the deceased--with rear of clothing cut away. Problem neatly solved.

When Olga called him to supper, he resented leaving work with only two parts of his grand plan finished. Olga said nothing more chatty than "More carrots?" during the entire repast. Ingle was too far lost in his dream to notice. (Ogla served him carrots at every meal-- including breakfast--in a moderately successful attempt to deal with Ingle's impressive volume of flatulence.)

After supper, Ingle nailed canvas strips to the coffin ceiling and tucked in sundry items such as hardtack. (Flour and water crackers so tough they were sometimes used as armor to deflect bullets.) He chose hardtack for its indestructibility. During the Civil War, soldiers ate--or tried to eat--hardtack left over from the Mexican War, which ended fifteen years earlier.

Olga announced her intention to retire for the evening. Ingle waved and offered an absent-minded, "Goodnight my dear." He chuckled to himself when a random thought occurred. A person must take great care with words. Only the trifling change of "r" to "d" separates "Dear" from "Dead."

Next to find a home in the canvas straps of the coffin lid came a silver flask of whiskey. After much deliberation, Ingle filled a second flask with wine. He preferred beer, but wine kept better. Including undrinkable Mississippi River water was quite unthinkable.

In the wee hours of the morning, Olga came downstairs in a disheveled state. Graying hair hung over her shoulder in a long, bedraggled braid. "Please, cannot hammering vait 'til morning? I cannot get ein vink of sleep."

"Of course, my dear." He switched from nails to horse-hoof glue.

At last he was ready for his stroke of genius, the innovation that would set his coffin above all others. This one key feature would propel him to the top of his profession and simultaneously elevate Olga to the uppermost ranks of the elite.

He fastened twenty-four canvas straps to the inside of the coffin lid, then unveiled his plunder from the Turner Hall.

During the Civil War, he had seen boys blowing into peculiar roundish balls used in a game they called "football." He blew up pig-innard-footballs until he was light-headed and his stomach ached from unaccustomed exercise to his diaphragm.

Ingle had paid twice their worth to secure two dozen of the leathery stomachs, the northside Turnverein's entire stock. Their life-saving potential made them well worth the price. When oxygen ran low, the undead would simply pull the plug on a football to release a new supply of air.

Last, Ingle contemplated what a person might need to make the wait worthwhile. What could be more comforting or instructive than Holy Scripture? But how to get light for reading?

Ingle pondered a number of possibilities--kerosene lamp, fireflies. But finally hit upon a miner's lamp along with flint and steel in a pewter case. With reflector and candle on the forehead, the occupant's hands would be free to turn pages.

Ingle added a few other touches to make the coffin more, well, homey. A blanket, a picture frame directly overhead to contain the image of a loved one, a backscratcher for those hard-to-reach itches, a magnifying glass for weak eyes.

By the time Olga awoke, he had nearly completed his magnum opus. He had even torn out and reset the bracing so as to limit the coffin width to three-and-one-half feet. Later, when the unneeded part had been sawed off, Muckenecker's Majestic would fit tidily in a standard grave plot.

Time for action. He rubbed his hands in anticipation. "Olga, bring the footstool. I need you to help me put the lid on the coffin. Fetch the maid too."

"You know maid not here so early."

"I think the two of us can manage." After they puffed and grunted the lid half on the coffin, he said. "Get in."

"Vhat? Get in coffin?"

He nodded and held out his hand to help her stand atop an ottoman. She heaved a sigh, climbed up and stepped in. The box lurched and nearly crashed. If he had not dropped to his knees to prop the box with his shoulder, the whole business would have toppled.

He steadied the mammoth box with his lower body as the pair of them tugged the lid over her. In seconds Olga began yelling up the pipe. "Gott in Himmel, let me out. Breathe I cannot. Futballs press mein bosom."

"Let the air out of them."

"Vhat? I cannot hear."

He spoke louder. "Pull out the stoppers. Open the corks."

"Vait, I get under pipe to hear."

When Olga shifted in the box, catastrophe struck. The box and Olga tumbled head down onto Ingle's chest which crushed him to the floor. When he found himself unable to inhale another single breath, he realized he was not long for this world.

He took comfort in one clear thought as he slipped away. My dearest Olga will prove Muckenecker's Majestic works. She shall be the richest widow in the state. My Olga will be the biggest society matron in the city.

He imagined exquisite adulation for himself in the eyes of his Olga. Inglefuss Muckenecker expired in the throes of an ecstasy both more haughty and more erotic than any he had ever known before.

"I cannot hear you, Ingle. Futballs press me so I cannot move. Not ring bells or toot vhistles. Downside up I am. Fumes iss fire in mein nose. Vine iss pouring on flints, and vhiskey iss soaking Mutter's Bible."

(Pause) Can you not hear me, Ingle? Picture of your Bruder iss pipe stopping up. You must make lid more high."

(Pause) She wheedled. "Ingle, let me out. Vool blanket give me rash, und magnifying glass stick me in mein eye."

(Pause) She adopted a pouting tone. "Schatzie, mein back itches vhere I cannot reach.

(Pause.) I have need of outhouse. Mein Schatz, torture me no more."

(Pause) Her voice surged in abrupt puffs strained with panic. "Ingle, liebe, iss you there?"

(Pause) Her voice came penitent and slow. "Mein liebling, mein lesson have I learned. You put me in box for I spend too much geld. I make you buy carriage and hire maid. No more. I promise not spend nothing vithout you say. I beg for each penny. Please, let me out."

(Pause) Her words dissolved into a pitiable low whine. "Please not to murder me. I fire maid. I scrub laundry on vashboard. I beg you let me out."

Her last words came in a wail sad enough to make angels weep. "Ingle, please. Futballs--futballs--in futballs I am smothering."

For more, visit: fedoraamis.com

GHOST MINE

Jud Minor
Second Place in the
Writer's Digest Short Story Contest

Amos leaned his bike against a hillside tree and glumly stared at the scene in front of him. A steep trail sloped down through the wooded hillside to the valley below. What had once been an incline railroad might now be an exciting 300-yard sled run, if anyone were brave enough to try it.

He thought, "*Why did I ever agree to this? This is dumb. Elves don't exist. That's stuff people believed in olden times. But this is 1938, not 1500. And even if they did exist, they wouldn't be hiding out in abandoned mines.*"

Halfway down the trail his new friends, slight-of-build Bobby, and boisterous Clarence, were waving to him.

"Come on, Amos!" Clarence shouted. "Let's get going."

As he stumped down the rocky path, he reflected on why he was doing this. He'd moved to this tiny western Pennsylvania Welsh mining village just three weeks ago, worried about how rural kids would take to a big city kid, and anxious to make friends. Clarence and Bobby had greeted him warmly. Then they took him on a Snipe hunt. Even though he knew it was a trick, he had played along. It was, they said afterwards, their initiation into their musketeers' club. He would be their third musketeer. Now they wanted to take him on an elf hunt. Oh brother, what next?

According to local folklore, Welsh elves were with the Welsh miners when they came over from the old country to mine coal. When the Great Depression forced the mines to close, the elves moved in. Clarence had discovered a mine that had not been boarded up. He was sure it would be a great place to look for the little people. Clarence and Bobby insisted Amos go along with them on their "really neat" new adventure. How could he refuse?

When he arrived where his friends were standing, Clarence grabbed his arm and pointed, "Look through the trees, Amos. See that rock shelf where the hill bends? There's a big ravine beyond it. The abandoned mine is at the far end. What a great place to find little people."

"Will I see little people here in the woods?" Amos asked in a disgusted tone.

"No, but I bet there are some in the mine," Clarence cheerfully replied.

After a five-minute walk the boys reached the rock shelf. Amos shuddered as he looked up the ravine. Its walls rose sharply. Ugly-looking clumps of vegetation clung to its jagged outcroppings. Some distance ahead, at the mouth of the ravine, piles of rubble gave the impression a mine was there.

"See it?" Clarence asked, gleefully clapping his hands.

"No," Amos snorted.

"Follow me. You'll see it when we get closer."

Halfway up the gorge Amos spotted what looked like a mine entrance. A dark opening in the hill was hidden behind dense underbrush. When they reached the mine, Bobby pushed aside some of the branches surrounding the opening and clicked on his flashlight. Its beam barely penetrated the dark, foreboding interior. Stale, clammy air greeted Amos as he peered over Bobby's shoulder. Heavy wooden roof beams held up by support timbers were spaced along its walls. Rusted rail tracks, half-covered by dirt and leaves, ran along the mine floor into its black depths. Cobwebs were everywhere.

"I hear water dripping," Amos announced. "I'm not going in there!"

"Gimme a break," Clarence replied. "We're the Three Musketeers. One for one! All for all!"

"That's one for all and all for one," corrected Amos. "My mom warned me about these old mines. They're dangerous."

Clarence snorted, "Amos thinks the Wild Welshman will get him. Are you afraid of the bogeyman? Is the bogeyman going to get you? Ha! Ha!"

Amos had heard the stories local hill folk liked to tell about the Ghost of the Wild Welshman. A boisterous Welsh miner had been trapped when his mine collapsed. His friends tried valiantly to dig him out, but his body was never recovered. Now, when anyone disappeared, hill folk would say the Wild Welshman got him. Amos had pretty well decided that story was just a tall tale, and that the little people didn't exist either. He couldn't understand why Bobby and Clarence believed those fairy tales.

"I don't believe that stuff," said Amos. "That's a made up ghost story."

"So what's your problem?" asked Clarence.

"Old mines aren't safe!"

Clarence countered, "This mine's been here a zillion years. If it was going to fall down, it would have by now. It's safe. Don't be chicken."

"Come on, Amos." Bobby added, "If it looks bad we can turn around."

"Okay! Okay!" Amos replied, not wanting to disappoint his new friends, "I'll go. But I think it's a dumb idea." He didn't admit his fear of the dark.

With flashlights on, they entered the darkness. Water dripping from somewhere splashed on Amos' hand and sleeve. Something buzzed by his face. He shuddered. The air reeked with the smell of mildew and rotting wood. The smell grew ever stronger as they walked further into the mine, leaving a bitter taste in Amos' mouth. The mine's coal- encrusted walls and gnarled support timbers soaked up most of the light from their flashlights, giving the tunnel a very sinister appearance.

They walked by a rusty mine car. It was empty except for a long metal rod sticking out. Beyond the cart they were forced to climb over a fallen roof timber. Then the mine curved sharply left. Several steps beyond the curve, Amos glanced back. To his horror he could no longer see the entrance. Utter blackness! The mine entrance had disappeared from view. With growing alarm he remembered years back, when he was trapped under his bed covers. His mother had tucked blankets tightly around him. During the night he had managed to get turned around. When he awoke his head was facing the foot of the bed. He started to crawl and immediately hit a dead end. He flailed and screamed. When his mother finally rescued him, it took forever to calm down.

"I'm leaving!" shouted Amos, fighting to control his panic.

He dashed out of the mine, heart pounding. Without stopping he ran to the front of the ravine, through the woods, and onto the old incline railroad path. There, he had second thoughts. What am I doing? *Get yourself under control, Amos. Don't leave your buddies. What if something awful happens to them?*

Back he went, muttering about stupid adventures and friends with no sense.

At the mine entrance he faintly heard Bobby's voice echoing down the shaft, "I'm trying, Clarence! I'm trying!"

Amos charged into the tunnel, past the mine car, over the fallen beam, and around the bend, tripping over the mine car track. What he saw when he reached his friends shocked him. Clarence was flat on his face, a large beam lying across his legs. Bobby was on his knees, flashlights beside him, trying to lift it. Beyond them several mine timbers were at sharp angles, partially blocking the tunnel.

Bobby looked up at Amos, sweat dripping from his forehead, "Am I glad you're back! Roof timbers began to fall. Clarence was ahead of me. He started back and tripped. This big beam landed on him. I can't lift it."

Together Amos and Bobby tried to budge the timber without success.

"I'm trapped forever!" wailed Clarence. "I'll die!"

"I've got an idea," exclaimed Amos. He ran back to the mine car and returned, dragging the long, rusty metal rod. "If we slide this rod under the beam, we can make a lever and lift."

They shoved the metal rod in place under the long end of the beam just beyond where it had pinned Clarence's legs. With their backs to Clarence they crouched, and heaved, Bobby holding the end of the rod and Amos next to him. They hoisted with all their might. To no avail! The beam didn't budge. As he struggled and strained, Amos looked down the partially blocked tunnel and tensed, shivers running down his spine. In its black depths the figure of a man materialized. He was wearing a miner's hat, knee-high boots, and a coat with torn elbows. He held a pickaxe in his hand. *A frightening thought flashed through Amos' brain. Is it the ghost of the Wild Welshman?*

In a voice that reverberated like the deep tones of a pipe organ, the apparition spoke, "You can do it, kid! Give it another heave."

Energy he never knew he had surged through Amos. He heaved, and with a creaking groan the big beam moved. Back straight, and legs tensed he strained and strained again. The coal encrusted timber lifted.

"I'm out! I'm out!" shouted Clarence, as he squirmed out from under the rough beam.

Bobby let go of the rod, turned, and knelt by Clarence.

"You okay?"

"I guess so. My legs really hurt."

Amos was transfixed by the being

he saw amongst the fallen timbers. As he stared, the apparition smiled. Then the miner began to fade. Amos held the rod tightly as he continued to stare into the now completely black tunnel, his mind in a whirl.

Bobby shouted, "What are you staring at? Let's get Clarence out of here!"

Amos released the rod. The beam crashed to the floor. Bobby retrieved fallen flashlights. They helped Clarence up, and placed his arms over their shoulders. Then the Three Musketeers headed for the entrance.

Once outside, Bobby looked intently at Amos, "How come, all of a sudden, you could lift that beam? And, what were you staring at back there?"

"Nothing, it's just..." Amos paused, trying to think what to say.

Clarence sighed as he studied his scraped legs, "You were right, Amos. That was a dumb idea. That's the last old mine I'll go into! So what did you see back there?"

Amos looked back at the mine entrance and winced. The apparition was standing there, just inside the mine entrance. The miner placed his forefinger across his mouth. *The ghost doesn't want me to tell!*

As the vision again disappeared, Amos inspected his rust-encrusted hands, and searched for an answer that would keep the secret. After a pause he grinned at his friends and said, "I thought I saw bats." Then he looked again at the mine entrance, his mind churning, *I should have been scared silly when that thing appeared, but I wasn't. I've got to come back here again.*

SCATTER NOT MY ASHES

Gemma P Geslani, PhD.
Taken from "In My Father's Footsteps."

Scatter not my ashes
into the ocean waves
for to the depths they'll settle
sunk by the grief I bear;
no chance of ever rising
to see your face again,
no chance of e'er escaping
that damp, eternal hell.

Scatter not my ashes
into the howling winds,
their wails will wilt my whispers
and you won't hear me when
I say how much I cherish
and miss you dearly still,
how much I wish a moment
with you I still can steal.

But strew my lifeless cinders
down soft a rolling hill,
where gaily sway white daisies
and golden daffodils,
and in those pretty flowers
my spirit e'er will dwell,
each time you kiss them tender
you'll kiss away my tears.

Scatter not my ashes
until with yours they're twilled
and to the Great Forever
forever we will sail
we'll blazon streaks of silver
the skies we cross where'er —
bright rays of our love's glory
to light our midnight trails.

@2019 Gemma P Geslani, PhD

On Rowing a Boat Down a Kansas Farm Road

Edward E Kindley

Your arms ache,
the boat moves grudgingly,
bottom scraping dirt and rock,
oars seeking hold in dry ditches
where only wild sunflowers
brighten the barren landscape;
not yet time for the cottonwoods
to add their layer of snow.
Here, nothing is easy.

Are you dreaming, or is this real?
the sun beating down, you drenched
in sweat, while the thunderclouds
gather, the sky turns its tornado-weather
yellow as you await the afternoon
hailstorm that is bound to come.

There is no shelter in the boat, unless
you turn it upside-down. But wait –
perhaps hail on the road will
make the rowing easier.

THE PARADE

Larry Lovan

The old man watched as the mayor finished his abbreviated speech, returned to his seat and slumped down. The mayor pulled off his straw hat and mopped his beet-red face with a handkerchief of about the same color. It was a futile gesture. The handkerchief was already saturated and sweat ran down his wrist and onto his shirt cuff. There was a large, dark stain in the back of his linen waistcoat. His Honor had earlier shed the jacket. The old man chuckled. The mayor was sweating like he was running for re-election.

It was hot on the reviewing stand. He wondered why someone hadn't enough sense to erect a cover over the stage. A canvas tarp would have worked nicely and been easy enough to install. It would have still been hot, but a covering would have gone a long way to lessen the intensity of the summer sun. But no one had thought of it, and why should they? They'd only scheduled this farce for noon on what was arguably the hottest day each year, July 4th. The oversight did have one unexpected benefit. It considerably shortened the usually long-winded harangues of the politicians. "Thank God for that," the old man said, not realizing he'd spoken aloud.

A trickle of sweat ran down the back of his neck. Dad-blasted wool uniform, stunk of mothballs too. He was seated off to one side, in the center of the second row, among the other guests of honor.

They were Plainsview's remaining American Civil War veterans. Oddly enough, their portion of the reviewing stand had been erected next to an old oak tree that provided them some shade. Still, it was hot.

He looked around at the other members of his group. Most of them looked like gol- danged idiots wearing their old worn, moth-eaten and ill-fitting uniforms. Gray hair and tangled beards, shriveled up, bent, clutching canes with wrinkled, trembling hands. He supposed he looked just as pathetic. He'd thought to avoid this particular embarrassment by wearing his Sunday best. On an earlier visit to his farm, he'd been urged by the committee in charge of this nonsense to be sure and wear his uniform. He'd responded by telling them he hadn't seen it in ages and had no idea where it was. Only half of that statement had been a lie. It was true he hadn't seen it in forever, but he knew where it was. The uniform was in Phyllis's cedar-chest, where it'd lain undisturbed for over half a century.

After the committee left, curiosity got the better of him and he opened the chest and took it out. It was in remarkably good shape and no doubt still fit. Yet he had no intentions of wearing it. It was in good shape because it was a new uniform. The cheap things didn't last anytime at all in the field. But this uniform had never seen the field. He'd been issued this uniform the day after the Grand Parade in Washington. Just like the army to give you a new uniform when you no longer needed one. In the parade, he'd worn his battered field dress, pants cuffs in tatters, right knee out with three multi-colored patches in the ass. The jersey had been little better—threadbare, torn and badly stained. At least he'd had a decent pair of shoes to march in. Still, he'd looked a lot like a scarecrow, which meant he fit right in with everyone else in Uncle Billy's Army of the Tennessee. They were all dressed in rags.

He got up this morning fully intending to don his Sunday suit. Instead, he pulled on the Union blue. Maybe that's the way it should be. It's what Phyllis would have wanted. She'd always been so proud of him. He'd have tossed this dern uniform fifty years ago, but she'd lovingly preserved it in her chest. Had she only been gone two years? Felt like a hundred. The uniform did fit.

The old man looked back at the rostrum where some other bombastic bag-of-wind was now boring the audience silly. Didn't the fool realize the audience was suffering in this heat just like they were? Didn't he realize no one gave a damn about anything he had to say? They were here to see the soldiers march. Start the parade already. Who is this blowhard anyway? The old man squinted at him. It was the district's federal Congressman. He'd voted against that pompous ass.

He went back to examining the group he was seated with. There were about a score of them. The committee had even managed to dig up a pair of Rebs. Now where in hell had they come from? Plainsview was right in the middle of Illinois and had been firmly Unionist in sympathy. Most likely they'd migrated here after the war, probably from Little Egypt. There'd been a lot of southern sympathizers down there. One Confederate was huge. He was dressed in an artillery tunic that he'd somehow managed to button. The old man wondered if it was split up the back. The Johnny had well combed gray hair and a neatly trimmed gray beard. He wore wire-rimmed glasses. His chubby hands were folded on top of his large gut.

The old man couldn't stop staring at him. He couldn't recall ever seeing a fat Confederate during the war. Rebs were all skin, bones, sinew and grit. This tub was big enough to make up a whole gun crew by himself. Obviously, he hadn't missed any meals in the last fifty years. So why'd his uniform still fit? Something was amiss here. He realized that the Reb was now staring back and none too friendly. Well, the hell with him. Maybe he'd spent the whole war sitting in a fort somewhere.

The old man turned his head and looked the other way, in the direction he'd been purposely avoiding. There, seated at the end of the first row, in the place of honor, closest to the dignitaries, was the Reverend Ward. Ward was dressed in an officer's uniform. He hadn't been a reverend during the war, although he'd argued that point, claiming he'd gotten his "calling" as a youth. He hadn't been an officer either, until late in the war when he'd volunteered for one of the Negro regiments. It was a quick way to become an officer, as well as a gentleman, as Negroes weren't allowed to hold rank higher than that of sergeant. Until then they'd served in the same company and the old man had outranked Ward, a fact that galled Ward to no end.

Ward was seated in his wooden wheelchair, totally oblivious to what was going on. Some drool ran down his chin and dripped onto his tunic. No oak tree shaded him but then no one was overly concerned about the sun frying Ward's brain. A massive stroke had already cooked it to a crisp some years before. The old man couldn't help but wonder what sort of God would blight a faithful servant with such a curse and leave him a vegetable— even if it was an improvement. He could hear his wife's voice in his head scolding him. *"Shame on you! Show some respect, he is a man of God for heaven's sake!"* He smiled and wiped his eyes with the back of his hand. The funny thing was, Phyllis never had any use for the Reverend Ward either. She could spot a fake as well as he could.

Now the congressman brought up a Colonel to introduce to the audience, which applauded and cheered. Good, maybe they were finally going to get the parade started. The Colonel was introduced as Colonel something or another, commanding the local National Guard Regiment. He had served valiantly in Cuba during the war with Spain. He'd served valiantly in the Philippines, during the Philippine Insurrection. In fact, he'd served valiantly everywhere he'd served. He had a chest full of ribbons to show just how valiant he was. The congressman assured the crowd that Colonel What's

It, was infinitely qualified to lead our local boys to victory over the Kaiser. If they believed those skirmishes qualified him to lead anyone anywhere, a lot of young men were going to die. But not the Colonel—he'd just accumulate more ribbons to enhance how valiant he was. If he'd had a gun on him, the old man would have considered shooting the stupid son of a bitch, along with the congressman.

The parade, once finally started, didn't last long as there was only one regiment marching. They were a gallant-looking bunch of soldiers—heads held high, chests thrust out, marching in perfect order. That was something the old man and his comrades had never been able to master. They sang as they marched, "Over there, over there..." It was a song the old man had never heard before, but it was a good song. One made for marching to and being sung by rough, virile voices. When they finished it and broke immediately into "The Battle Hymn of the Republic," the old man felt a twinge deep in his chest. That song had belonged to him and his companions. They struggled to their feet to stand in honor.

He shifted his gaze to the audience. Fathers, who should have known better, were eagerly hoisting their infant sons onto their shoulders to see. Mothers, whose instincts should have warned them, were waving handkerchiefs and feigning heartache as their darling sons marched by. The pretty girls pushed their way to the front where they stood blushing and throwing flowers. And the soldiers: the sons, brothers, husbands, fathers, lovers, beamed with pride and marched straighter still.

The old man felt sick.

Afterwards, the committee hauled the veterans over to the fairgrounds for the annual picnic. They did it in fine fashion, transporting them in fancy motor carriages all decked out with red, white and blue bunting. Of course none of the carriages had roofs to protect them from the searing sun or the clouds of dust the vehicles kicked up.

Upon arrival at the fairgrounds they were shunted off to a bunch of tables set a ways off from the rest, as everyone had pretty much lost interest in them by then. That was fine with the old man. They were placed near the creek, under the shade of several towering sycamore and elm trees. He really didn't think he'd have much of an appetite after what he'd witnessed, but he surprised himself. He downed several pieces of fried chicken, some potato salad, beans and a couple of glasses of lukewarm lemonade.

No one at the table said much. Most of them were hard of hearing anyway. It was quite pleasant, as long as you didn't look at the head of the table. That was where the committee had parked the Reverend/Captain Ward. Several ladies from his church were trying to feed him, getting more food on him than in him. The old man wondered if they changed his diapers, too.

Dessert was brought over and with it came the editor of the local newspaper. With pencil and pad ready, he worked his way down the table wanting to know what advice they had for the "doughboys."

"Always listen to and obey your officers," said the obese Rebel, to a chorus of snorts from the veterans nearest him. "They're the ones who know what's going on." That brought several derisive laughs from the table. *Knew it,* thought the old man, *he's a phony*.

Someone else said, "The soldiers should remember that they are Americans and Christians," whatever the hell that meant.

The only one who had any sensible advice was Private Patrick Murphy, who was seated across from, and just to the right of the old man. "Aim low and shoot to kill," he said.

The editor wrote that on his pad with a serious scowl on his face, nodding his head up and down like he'd just been let in on a big secret.

"And shoot only enlisted men. Don't waste your bullets on officers."

The editor jerked his head up. "Shoot only at enlisted men?" Murphy nodded his head. "Why so?"

"Because they're the ones trying to kill you." The editor stared at him for a moment, then shrugged his shoulders and wrote that bit of commonsense down, too. Finished, he looked across the table. "And what about you, old timer?" he asked with a smarmy, condescending smile. "I'm sure a sergeant would have some good advice for our boys?"

The old man nodded his head. "That I do," he said.

When he didn't elaborate the editor asked, "Well, would you share it with us?"

"Gladly. Desert."

That wiped the smile off the editor's face and replaced it with a look of shock, an honest emotion at last. It also brought chuckles from several of the veterans and an "Amen," from Murphy. The editor didn't record any of this. Instead, he turned and hurried away.

They drove the old man back home in another motor car and deposited him on the steps of his farmhouse just before dark. He fetched his pipe and a jug and settled in the ancient rocking chair on his front porch so he could watch the fireworks. The chair had once belonged to his grandmother. His old tomcat took its place on his lap, and he ran one gnarled, veined hand over its head and scratched behind its ear.

One of the advantages of living in a flat state like Illinois was that you could see forever. Even though the fairgrounds were a good half dozen miles away, he'd have an unimpeded view. It was like watching a thunderstorm in the distance. There'd be a bright flash and eventually a rumble. He and Phyllis had watched them many a time over the years.

He knew there'd be no sleep tonight. Too many memories had been awoken. Too many ghosts set to stirring. He felt his eyes fill with tears and then start to track down his cheeks. Those poor fools, they had no idea what they were letting themselves in for. He took a drink and remembered.

THE AMERICAN DREAM

Laura Stewart Schmidt

*U*NKNOWN CALLER, said the ID.

Toby swore. Another creditor? But they didn't usually call in the middle of the night, even if you owed them thousands of dollars.

And Toby owed a lot of people a lot of money.

UNKNOWN CALLER gave up. Thank God.

She got up and turned on the porch light for her mother. Mom's ceramics class ran until nine-thirty, then she usually went for coffee with friends. Maybe one of the Silver Foxes, as Mom's group of friends called themselves, had some pressing problem to discuss.

As if that bunch of fifty-somethings had problems. They were all stable and steady as the Pentagon.

Except Mom. She was probably the one bending everyone's ear tonight. *I can't get my irresponsible failure of a kid out of my house. Thirty going on three. Broken marriage, broken career, broken credit. Broken. Why don't I just throw her out like I would anything else that's broken?*

Bam-bam-bam!

Toby almost jumped out of her skin. Banging on the door at almost midnight? That couldn't be anything good.

She looked through the peephole. Two county police officers stood at the door.

Oh, my God. I'm going to jail.

She grasped the doorknob with

shaking hands and opened the door.

"Roberta Shelton?" one of the officers said.

She brought her hands together and held them out. "Yes."

The officer didn't go for his handcuffs. "May we come in?"

It wasn't like she had a choice.

It occurred to Toby that Mom might be shocked if she came home to find the police in her house just as she realized Mom should have been home long ago. Then the first officer cleared his throat and said, "Ma'am, there's been an accident."

She had to identify the body. Her first thought when she looked down at the still, silent shell was, *I guess this makes me an orphan*.

"Is there anyone we can call for you?" one of the officers asked.

Toby gave her head a little shake. "Uhm…" She had no living relatives nearby. She'd been an only child, as had her father, who'd passed away when she was in high school. "My best friend."

"What's her number?"

"His." Toby fished her phone out of her purse and found Mike's number. "Mike Caniff."

The officer peered at the screen. "501? Where's that?"

"Arkansas, just west of the Bootheel. We had a farm near Walnut Ridge when I was a child and that's where I met Mike…" She trailed off. The officer had that *I'm sympathetic but I wish you would stop babbling look*.

She needed Mike. She didn't know where to begin planning a funeral. And unless Mom had life insurance, she would have a pauper's burial.

But Mom did have life insurance, enough to cover the cost of the funeral and burial. She also left her house and a savings account to Toby.

Mike left his construction business and drove up from Arkansas for the funeral and reading of the will. He greeted Toby's discovery that she was no longer broke with much less shock than she did. "Who else would your mom leave her money to?"

"The animal shelter? The Sierra Club? Mike, come on. You know how disappointed she's been with me."

"Disappointed in how things have worked out for you."

Toby leaned against the back of the sofa and closed her eyes. "She and Dad have been frustrated with me since Day One. They wanted me to be something productive. An unpublished poet doesn't qualify." She didn't add her suspicion that they'd sold the beloved family farm to punish her. They'd known how much she loved it. That she wanted to live there someday.

"There's nothing wrong with being a poet." Mike's strong hand rested on her shoulder blades.

Toby snorted. "If she saw me writing, she gave me the same look as when Bruce took me for a ride. Believe me, she wasn't angry at Bruce. She was angry at me for falling for his crap."

Toby's ex-husband had taken one look at her mother's colonial home and fallen in love. He'd done a remarkable job of convincing Toby it was with her. The reality, that he needed a well-heeled woman to support him, hadn't come out until several years and a dozen maxed-out credit cards later.

Then there was the house.

Toby had made the down payment. Bruce torched it to get the insurance money. The investigator figured out his game, so not only did he fail, but he was charged with insurance fraud. (Not arson. It was perfectly legal to destroy your own property.) Then Bruce disappeared, and Toby, who had lost everything she owned in the fire, still owed the finance company for a house that wasn't there anymore.

That was two years ago. She was still getting collection letters.

"I don't think so." Mike's gentle voice brought Toby out of the nightmarish reverie.

"She told me not to marry him. I thought I knew better."

Mike tried to laugh. "I don't have anything to say, since I'm in the middle of a divorce."

Toby nodded. Mike had called her crying the day he received the papers. "How's it going?"

"How does a divorce always go? At least we didn't have kids or property to fight over. She'll quitclaim the house. Dinah goes her way, I go mine."

Toby made a sympathetic noise.

"You know, you could pay off everybody you owe now."

"No."

"You can't?"

"I won't. I don't want to use all Mom's money to pay off the mortgage on the house I don't have. Or the credit cards, which are full of Bruce's bar bills and stuff he bought for his girlfriends. He left me holding the bag, and it weighs as much as Alaska. I'm sick of it."

"What about bankrupt—"

She shook her head before he'd finished the sentence. "I already talked to a lawyer about that. It won't wipe out everything, and it'll wreck my credit for years." She had to laugh. "My *credit*. Which is already a wreck."

"It might be worth it just to put some of this behind you."

She had to make Mike understand. "This is the first break I've had. I want to go back to Walnut Ridge. I can't get the farm back, but I can buy a house in town, and have something that's mine. No one can come along and garnish it or seize it."

"But they will," Mike said. "Unless you get those debts taken care of, as soon as you buy something, they'll come along and snap it up."

"Not if it's in your name."

♦ ♦ ♦

Finding the perfect house was easy. She remembered a block of old Victorian homes in Walnut Ridge; two, and three-story houses with wraparound front porches, balconies, awnings and gingerbread. Even the name fit—Aldersgate.

She found one for sale. To say it was in disrepair would be massively understating the issue. No one had lived in it or cared for it for almost three years. The front porch railing sagged, the shutters were warped and rotting, and several broken windows had let in mice, rain and leaves. Inside was worse. Boxes and stacks of moldy newspapers filled the corners, and the odor of decay and animal urine hung in the air.

Toby and Mike went to work. Mike donated the services of several employees. Armed with surgical masks and Vicks VapoRub, they carried out boxes, hauled newspapers to the recycling bin, and vacuumed nest material and leaves. Mike's guys scrubbed and painted with the soft colors Toby had chosen, and by the time she (or rather, Mike) had owned the house for three weeks, the inside walls gleamed lemon and lilac, and the outside matched the sky on the sunniest day, with dusty rose shutters. The rest of the money bought carpeting, furniture and curtains, and delivery trucks jockeyed for space on the shady street.

"What's this room going to be?" Mike asked as he vaulted over the edge of a first-floor French window. The lock didn't work, but Toby didn't care. Who needed locking windows in Walnut Ridge?

Toby smiled. "My writing studio. Watch your feet on the carpet."

"Are you here for good?"

"Not yet. I'll spend tonight here, then I have to go back to St. Louis and finish moving out of Mom's house."

"Are you going to leave this place sitting?"

"You could stay here. It's your house, after all."

Mike gave her a one-armed hug. "I'll keep an eye on it. You might want to think about an alarm system. You've put a lot of money into this place, and I'd hate to see anything happen to wreck your dream."

"Me, too." She picked a piece of dirt off her t-shirt. "If you hadn't done this, I would have lost everything Mom left me."

He grinned. "Things are looking up for you, Toby. I feel it."

She'd sold Mom's house quickly to an upscale young couple thrilled to get a place so close to their new law office. She packed as much as she could fit into a U-Haul and figured the rest could go to Goodwill. She was doing a final walk-through, checking for anything of monetary or sentimental value, when her cell rang.

PRIVATE NUMBER. Great. Another creditor. Well, maybe she'd just pay this one off. "Hello?" Her voice echoed in the almost-empty house.

"Toby? This is Dinah Caniff."

Toby started. "Hello, Dinah." She hadn't spoken to the woman in months.

"I've got some bad news." Dinah's voice was brisk and businesslike. "Mike was in an accident at work. He's dead."

"What?" Toby whispered.

"He fell off a ladder."

"A ladder?"

"Yes. He was finishing up a job near Pocahontas, and his ladder broke."

"Broke?"

Dinah *tsk'd*. "Do you understand anything I said?"

"Dead? Mike is dead?"

"Yes."

Toby tried not to breathe, as though that might

make the whole conversation imaginary, a dream, a nightmare.

"There's going to be a memorial service Thursday," Dinah went on. "I'll text you the information if you want to come."

Yes, of course she would go. Because that would show none of this was real.

"You'll want to find a place to stay here. I'd put you up at Mike's, but I'm going through all his things."

"I have a house I'm moving to," Toby murmured, wiping her face with her palm.

"I have to clear out our old place so I can sell it," Dinah said. "I'm going to live in his new house."

Toby froze, tears drying cool and itchy on her cheeks, hand poised at her nose. "What did you say?"

"Mike fixed up one of those big houses on Aldersgate. A blue-and-pink three-story."

"You can't live there." Toby forgot her grief in a flash of sick panic. "That's my house. I bought it!"

"Then why is Mike's name on the deed?"

"That's a technicality. It's mine. We put it in Mike's name so I wouldn't lose it to my ex-husband's creditors."

Silence. Then, "You'll have a hard time proving that."

"Proving it to who? You? Dinah, you've known me as long as you've known Mike. My mother just died and—"

"Mike told me." *I'm sorry* might have been nice.

Toby's words gushed. "She left me enough money to buy that house. I've wanted to move to Walnut Ridge since I was a kid and my family had that farm. Mike helped me fix up the house. You can ask anyone who knows him. He lent me his crew to work on it. You know he wouldn't have put pink shutters on his own house!"

"What's your point?"

Toby stared at the phone. "Well, I, I mean, it, it's my house, Dinah. You can have the one on Roe Street—"

"Don't tell me where I can live." The words hit Toby like a spray of icy hail. "I'll tell you where I'm going to live. That house on Aldersgate. It was in Mike's name, and when he died, I inherited it. I suggest you buy yourself another house."

She couldn't even figure out how to kill herself.
She didn't own a gun.
Sleeping pills didn't even make her drowsy.
Poison would be too painful. There had been enough pain lately. The farm, Bruce, Mom, Mike...and now, her beautiful house. Her perfect house.
Her house.
She spent the rest of the evening sobbing into a handful of paper towels that scraped her skin raw. At three-thirty she threw her things in the car and got on the highway for Arkansas. What was the point in staying? Although, really, what was the point in going? There was nothing for her there either. No house, no Mike.
No Mike.
Mike had been doing construction since he was a teenager. What would have made him climb a defective ladder?
His death at this time was too much of a coincidence. Mike hadn't had a chance to do any legal paperwork to ensure the house would go to Toby if anything happened to him. There was only one person who benefitted from his death, and that was Dinah—who hardly sounded like a grieving widow.
What had Dinah done?
Toby arrived in Walnut Ridge at seven a.m. She checked into a motel and sat down on the double bed with a rental brochure. Dinah was right about one thing. Toby had to find a place to live.
Then she would find out what really happened to Mike.

She rented a small furnished apartment, barely big enough for her collection of books and back issues of *Poets & Writers*. The sand-colored stains in the bottom of the bathtub wouldn't come off no matter how much Comet she used. A series of nail holes in the living room still smelled faintly of the Colgate someone had used to patch them.

But it was someplace, and it was in Walnut Ridge, and she was home. Sort of.

She drove around town one day, depositing resumes and filling out applications, in case anyone in a town of 4000 people might have a use for a writing major. Finn's Market did, and Toby got a job sweeping the floors and taking out the trash.

On her off days, she plotted how she could expose Dinah. If Dinah had rigged the ladder to break, someone might have seen her at the house on Roe Street, Mike's house, where he kept all his work equipment in his shed. Maybe she had left some clue.

Toby had a key to the Roe Street house. She also had keys to the Aldersgate house, of course, but Dinah had probably changed the locks.

But maybe Dinah hadn't done anything about the window that didn't lock.

◆ ◆ ◆

Toby went to the Roe Street house on her next day off. If anyone asked, she would have told them Mike borrowed a tool from her when they were working on the new house and she needed it back. In keeping with the story, she pocketed a long aluminum wrench.

She wasn't sure what she'd hoped to find. But there was nothing in the garage. The broken ladder had been thrown out after the investigation into Mike's fall, and none of the three remaining ladders seemed damaged.

How could Dinah have known which ladder Mike would use?

Toby's head ached like someone

had kicked her. If Dinah had done something to the ladder to make Mike fall, she had gotten away with it. She would continue to get away with it unless Toby could trick her into confessing.

She headed over to Aldersgate and tried her key. It didn't fit. But the window hadn't been fixed, and she opened it and climbed into her writing room. Her shoes dropped bits of mud onto the ivory carpet.

I'll have to havc it cleaned.

"What are you doing here?"

Toby looked up to see Dinah pointing a gun at her. She froze.

She hadn't thought about Dinah being there, or how it would feel to have a gun looking at her. "It's my house."

Dinah laughed. "Are you still making that noise? This is not your house. Get out before I shoot you and tell the police you broke in."

"You killed Mike," Toby blurted.

Dinah stared. "What?"

"You did something to the ladder so he would fall. He must have told you I'd bought this house and you decided you wanted it."

"You're crazy." Dinah's hand holding the gun was steady. "But you're right about one thing. I knew about the house. Mike told me. He said if I came back to him, we would live here."

"Liar!"

Dinah shrugged. "Believe what you want."

She was making it up. She had to be. Mike wouldn't have betrayed Toby like that. He wouldn't have stolen her house from her.

But now she would never know.

Toby pulled the wrench out of her back pocket and flung it in Dinah's face.

Dinah shrieked and fired. The shot missed Toby by several feet. She rushed Dinah, the element of surprise on her side, and yanked the gun from the other woman's hands.

The second shot didn't miss.

They called it premeditated murder. She had no defense, no right to be in the house. Nor to have the stolen wrench, which was also Dinah's property. The prosecution painted her as an enraged former lover. No one believed her story.

Her leftover money was quickly swallowed by her attorney, who advised her to plead guilty. She refused, hoping the jury would understand.

They didn't. They recommended life in prison.

"All I wanted was a place of my own," she told the bailiff who led her away. "Something no one could take away from me. Isn't that everyone's dream?"

THE END

For more, visit: laurastewartschmidt.com

THE BOW
A Personal Essay

Gregory Lamping

"**I**'m going to see James Dickey, the guy who wrote Deliverance. You want to come?" I asked my brother Ralph, who had just knocked and was standing in the doorway of my two-room basement apartment. The poet and novelist was giving a poetry reading that evening at Drury College in Springfield, Missouri. It was November, 1973.

"Nah, it's starting to rain," Ralph said, on entering my apartment. Neither of us owned cars or umbrellas or raincoats, and the college was two miles away.

"Sorry, but I'm leaving," I said, slipping on my jacket.

"Mind if I stay?" Ralph asked, none too eager to face the rain again.

"Sure, go ahead, you can look at this," I said, tossing him the latest Playboy magazine. "There's an interview with James Dickey."

I had just bought the magazine. Though I was a student of literature, I had never read any of his poems, but on reading the interview, I thought, damn, I need to check this guy out.

James Dickey, an avid bow hunter, was asked in the interview why he chose to hunt the deer with a bow, rather than stalk it with a camera. He replied, "It's not the same. I would rather enter into the deer's universe of life and death, than stalk him for something as inconclusive as a photo. It's more of a tribute to the deer to join him on his own ground. It's his territory, not yours."

I couldn't imagine T.S. Eliot saying that. Here was a man who knew how survival plays out, who was engaged with the natural world and wasn't afraid to grab it with his bare hands.

When I stepped outside the front door of my apartment, I thought, yikes, my brother wasn't kidding. It wasn't just raining; it was pouring. I considered going back inside to get a trash bag to poke my head through for a makeshift rain poncho, but thought, no, better not. That would look stupid.

After walking fifty or so yards, I was soaked. My jeans probably gained a pint of water, while my blue corduroy jacket must have, oh god, soaked up a quart. What bothered me wasn't the sogginess of my clothes, but the stinging of the cold hard raindrops against my face. At times I could convince myself that nothing was unpleasant if I embraced a Zen mind and diverted my attention, but getting blasted by the rain was just too painful for me to ignore. My one consolation was that I couldn't get any wetter.

Trudging down Kimbrough Avenue, I saw lots of cars driving past me, but not a single pedestrian other than myself. The passing motorists must have thought that my car had broken down, since no one in his right mind would dare choose to be out in this rain.

Once I finally arrived on campus, it stopped raining (of course!). Wandering through a maze of sidewalks, I asked a student on her way to class the whereabouts of the Wilhoit Theater. "You're there," she said, looking over at the large building closest to us.

Entering the theater, I took a seat in the third row off to the side, stretching my arms along the backs of the seats at my sides. The theater soon began filling up with college students arriving in small groups. No one chose to sit within two seats of me, probably because

I looked like a homeless person who had just come in from the rain with my tousled, shoulder-length, stringy wet hair and drenched-to-the-bone clothes. I slouched in my seat waiting for the show to begin.

He stepped up on to the stage wearing a heavy fur coat hanging past his knees and a wide-brimmed Boss of the Plains beaver felt hat. He was a big man, six-foot-three and burly as a Kodiak brown bear. All eyes were fixated on him as he lumbered toward the lectern. I thought he was drunk or pretending to be drunk. He stood behind the lectern with his head down, as if trying to figure out what to do, before turning to take off his hat and place it on the chair at his side. He then slowly took off his coat, muttering, "I suppose it's not that cold in here." A few of us laughed, since we were wondering why he was wearing such a massive fur coat in such unwintry weather. After draping his coat over the chair, he went back to the lectern, looked up at us, and smiled.

James Dickey began by telling us a story. He said the other night he was lying in bed in a hotel room in Paris when he got a phone call from within the hotel. In mimicking the voice of the caller, James Dickey sounded like some cotton-balls-in-the-mouth, groggy drunk. The caller mumbled something about what's going on, why are you here? Dickey asked if we could guess the caller.

"Marlon Brando!" someone cried out from the back. James Dickey flashed a wide toothy smile and said, "You're right!"

Once he got that name-dropping bit out of the way, he was ready to start his reading. The first poem he chose was his well-known poem: "Falling." It was too long to read in its entirety, so he read to us the beginning. He explained that it was based on a true story he had once read in the *New York Times*, about a 29-year-old stewardess who had fallen to her death after being swept out of an emergency exit door that had suddenly sprung open on an airplane. Her body was later found in a cornfield by a farmer. The poem speculated on what might have gone through her mind as she was falling.

That's all I remember about the poem, his introduction. What I remember well, however, was his reading of the poem. His focus and delivery were vivid, heartfelt, and affecting. I was watching his facial expressions while listening to his words, though I was also listening to the sounds of his words, which were as poetic as their meaning.

The next one he read was another well-known poem: "The Firebombing." Again, it was a poem that was too long for him to read in its entirety. He based this poem on his World War II experience of having flown 80 combat missions in the Pacific Ocean theater as an airman in the 418th Night Fighter Squadron. In the poem, the narrator, a bomber pilot, never sees the terror and pain of the incendiary bombs he drops on the Japanese civilians below, only the lit-up nighttime beauty of the explosions. The poem begins ...

Homeowners unite.

All families lie together, though some are burned alive.

I can't say I remember much about this poem either. I was so anti-war at the time, having grown up during the horrors of the Vietnam War, that all I could think was, "Did James Dickey really kill all those people?"

Once he had finished reading his final poem for the evening and thanked us for coming, we erupted in applause. We could tell from his bright eyes and smile that he was proud of his poetry. He kept looking at us, basking in our appreciation, savoring the veneration, when he looked over and spotted ... me.

Who the hell is this? I imagined him thinking. I was this guy sitting off to the side, no one next to him, smiling and clapping. My hair was a mess and my clothes were clinging to me as if a giant wet dishrag had been flung against my body. James Dickey was probably wondering, *did this guy trudge through the pouring rain just to see ... me?*

I kept smiling and clapping and he kept smiling and looking at me. I felt as if I were in the spotlight with everyone wondering who James Dickey was staring at and why. I was embarrassed, yet flattered, wishing he would stop staring, but then, wishing he wouldn't. I could sense that he was looking at me because he believed that I was a die-hard fan of his poetry, and not just some bored English major with nothing better to do, that I had weathered a storm to see him.

He then stepped back from the lectern and turned to put his coat and hat back on with the assistance of a short man with a beard who I assumed to be an English professor at the college. As we continued clapping, James Dickey started walking across the stage, but this time with a steadier gait. He was near the end of the stage when he suddenly stopped and turned to look down at me. With our eyes locked, he placed his hand against his belly and bent his shoulders toward me. I thought, wow, James Dickey is acknowledging me with a bow! One of America's greatest living poets! A genius! The one who wrote that memorable movie line, "If he tries anything, I'll blow his dang-blang balls off."

On leaving the campus, I got lost again (of course!) and had to double back on a sidewalk meandering between two buildings and a grove of trees. I saw three shadowy figures coming towards me. The person on my left was a young woman with long, dark hair, who I could see even in the shadows, was strikingly beautiful. The person on my right was that bearded man I had earlier seen up on stage. And between them was big James Dickey.

My imagination quickly sized up the situation. James Dickey was focused on the poet groupie following alongside him. His head was turned toward her as he said her name and asked, "Are you a student here?" She flirtatiously flipped a wisp of hair from her face and said something softly, as if trying to sound like an ethereal beauty from a Pre-Raphaelite painting. The English professor, meanwhile, was facing straight ahead, playing the escort, but knowing that his services were no longer desired. I suppose it's possible that the girl could have been tagging along hoping to spend the rest of the evening listening to the great poet recite his poetry, but I don't think so, considering how many famous male poets had behaved given this situation.

I later read in *Summer of Deliverance*, a memoir of James Dickey by his son, Christopher, that his father was a philanderer who took advantage of poet groupies and faculty wives during his college reading tours, and that the poet's wife Maxine was a cirrhotic alcoholic who remained at home drinking every evening until she passed out, while her husband was miles away entertaining his admirers.

In that same book, I read that James Dickey was also a heavy drinker. On the first page, Christopher said that when he left home, his father ... *was drunk for most of those twenty years. If I didn't get him on the phone before eleven in the morning, there was no point in calling at all. He wouldn't remember, or couldn't speak coherently. And he never called me.*

Looking back on that evening, I believe James Dickey had been drinking and wasn't just pretending to be drunk, and that he probably later tried to have sex with that young woman with the long hair, and that he played the jackass at many a literary party by getting uproariously drunk and mouthing off insults and bellowing lines from *Deliverance*, but I also believe that he loved poetry more than anything else, and that his finest moments came in the writing of his poetry. In his book of self-reflection, *Sorties*, he wrote, "What you have to realize when you write poetry, or if you love poetry, is that poetry is just naturally the greatest goddamn thing that ever was in the whole universe."

He also wrote that during his poetry readings, he would sometimes look out into the audience and spot a face he believed reflected that same love of poetry that he felt toward his art.

THE WEDDING CAKE

Ross Braught

Long ago when swords and flying carpets were common and when magic was a household word there lived a magician, his wife, and their son. They lived in a small village surrounded by snowcapped mountain peaks. Unlike his father, the boy, whose name was Paul, never practiced magic.

One day the miller's son, whose name was Jeff, got married in the stone church in the center of the village. Paul's mother invited the couple over for dinner the same evening.

Suddenly Paul's mother realized that there was no wedding cake in the house and nothing to make one out of.

"Paul!" she exclaimed. "Our guests will have to have a cake and we don't even have a cup of flour in the house."

"Father will be returning in a week," said Paul. "He can easily make a cake out of his magic powders."

"Our guests must have a cake tonight!" replied his mother. "You shall mix your father's magic powders together and make a cake."

"But I've never used magic in my life," pleaded Paul.

"Then it's high time you learned some magic," said his mother. "I want the cake finished by this evening."

Paul opened the cupboard and examined the bottles of magic

potions and powders. Some of the bottles contained no labels, others had tags with illegible scrawls on them. Still others were neatly labeled but contained nothing worthwhile in making a cake. One such bottle had a liquid in it that would cure mumps. Another bottle contained a powder that would make flying carpets go faster.

Paul closed the cupboard doors with disgust and called for the family servant.

"Tell the guests to come early," he told the servant.

"Also tell them to bring flour, sugar, or any other cake ingredient with them."

A few minutes later Paul stepped outside the cottage, scaring Peter, the family's coal-black cat. The servant was already well beyond their garden plot and presently disappeared from view behind a group of evergreen trees. Paul heard someone talking inside the cottage, and, apparently having never learned that it is wrong to stand and eavesdrop behind closed doors, listened to his mother muttering to herself.

"That boy had better get back in here and start mixing magic powders and herbs," she was saying. "If that cake isn't made tonight, and I mean made perfectly, our family is disgraced."

Paul sighed and after dislodging Peter from the inside of his buttoned coat, rose and walked down the path leading to the garden. The cat followed at a respectful distance, meowing and making his usual assortment of odd noises. Peter had the bad habit of sharpening his claws on people's legs and was mostly kept outside. Paul kept a wary eye behind him as he walked along the uneven stone path that ended suddenly beside a large vegetable garden. Peter came running up, but he only pressed his head against Paul's trousers and meowed gloomily.

"Me and you, both," said Paul, recognizing the cat's melancholy mood.

Standing on the rise of ground beside the garden, he could see all the mountains that ringed the valley.

Evergreen trees, their boughs laden with wet snow, covered the mountainsides. Only the very tops of the tallest mountains were treeless. Everywhere else the graceful pine with its long sweeping branches and pungent odor had given life to an otherwise bleak winter landscape. Looking above the trees, Paul saw several sagging shapes drift over the peak of the nearest mountain. They were either clouds or magicians on their flying carpets, but he was too far away to tell which. Being a magician's son he had heard a lot of talk about such magic equipment. He had the idea that at the end of a long day's use, a flying carpet will sag and dip in its flight like a tired bird flapping back to her nest with one last evening tidbit for her young.

"I'd just as well walk," he said to the cat, who cocked an ear in return. "Sure the flying carpet gets you where you want to go faster. But if you shoot over the snowy mountains, you never get to walk beneath the pine boughs and smell the forest. Our servant doesn't have a flying carpet. And yet, I bet he is already in the village telling the guests to come early and bring some flour and sugar."

He paused and looked down at Peter. The cat had been his outdoor companion for several years, ever since his father had brought home a small kitten given to him by another magician. Paul often wondered if the cat would do anything magical, but fortunately the only mysterious happenings since the cat's arrival were the disappearance of a few pats of butter and the evaporation of a quart or two of milk. When it was cold in winter, Peter would meow at the front door and Paul would let him sit by the fireplace with a saucer of milk.

A breeze sprang up, causing a small shower of pinecones in a nearby woods. Paul shivered a little and returned to the cottage. Peter remained where he was, sniffing the air and purring to himself. As Paul got near the cottage he noticed that there was something different about it, especially about the air around it. He couldn't figure out what was absent, until he realized that there was no smell of baking in the air. In the past, there had always been the odor of baking bread and smoking sausages coming out of the cottage. The snow had been heavy the week before and his mother had missed her shopping. Paul stepped inside the cottage and quietly shut the door.

The sun, a brilliant display of red and amber, was quite low in the sky when the guests started arriving. Paul got out his mother's old cookbook with the faded cover. From the outside it looked exactly like his father's book of magic.

The first guest was the old blacksmith's wife who lived by the town mill. She brought two cups of butter with her. Paul's mother was so glad to see the old lady that she failed to notice the butter.

Paul took the butter and mixed it with a pound of flour that the town baker brought with him. The wooden spoon Paul held twirled around and around in the bowl.

The next guest to arrive was a little old lady who lived on the far side of town with chickens and goats. She had brought a dozen eggs.

Paul broke the eggs and beat them and beat them until his arms were tired. Then he turned the page in the cookbook.

"He's finally practicing magic," said the boy's mother, thinking he was reading a magic book. "I knew he'd take after his father."

The others were awed, too. They had been too busy talking to each other to notice that each of the guests had brought along an ingredient. They thought he was using magic to make a cake.

Then Paul poured the sugar that the tailor brought into the bowl of eggs and beat them with the wooden spoon until the mixture was like heavy cream. Having done this, he poured the flour and butter mixture into the sugar and egg mixture. He beat this until his arms were quite sore. Then he poured this into a greased pan and heated it in a warm oven.

The cake had been baking for quite a while when a knock came on the door. It was Jeff, the miller's son, and his bride Mary, daughter of the town barber. They quickly came in and shut the door, closing out the thick night fog. The guests all crowded around the couple and congratulated them.

Paul pulled the cake out of the oven and set it on the table. It was a beautiful cake and its top had been sculpted into mountains, valleys, and streams. The guests gasped when Paul took a large wooden star and placed it on top of the largest mountain.

"I didn't know that you were a magician, Paul," said Jeff. "But this cake was plainly made by magical means."

Mary, his bride, got the piece with the wooden star.

"This star is certainly magic," she said. "May I keep it?"

"Certainly," said Paul. "You may also have the leftover cake."

When the party was over the guests thanked Paul and his mother and left.

As the years passed and Paul grew older he became better and better at accomplishing simple chores. Even though he never rode a flying carpet his neighbors called him a magician.

The End

Immigrant Christmas 1947

Virginia Renz Higgins

Her hands place the pinecone garland on the tree branches with care, making sure the rows are straight and evenly spaced. It is the same clumsy strand from their first Christmas in America, made with the small pinecones collected from the side yard. They'd been as giddy as children, amazed at the bounty their own yard afforded, as though the pinecones represented yet another of America's seemingly ceaseless offerings. She had woven red yarn in and around each one, making a strong net to hold the crusty orbs in place. Time had made them especially brittle, and her care with the garland this last Christmas Eve was an attempt to preserve something she held precious.

There had been so much hope within them in those long-ago years, when the best of life seemed to lie ahead. They had no way of knowing the bitterest of disappointments awaited them, that there would never be children, that their family was already complete. *Keine Kinder*. Their lack was observed by friends and neighbors in this country of openness and curiosity, and they were often asked whether children were planned or hoped for. To plan for them would mean to deny the facts; but the hope, through whatever intervention God could devise, had lingered.

Hilde had wanted candles on that first tree as it had been done when she was a child. This was not his memory, as he had come from Stuttgart, where the *Weihnachtsbäume* were decorated with nuts and dried fruits. Otto worried about fire, but gave in to the tradition of her little town on the Rhine River. At last, when the final candle was lit, they turned off the lamps and sat together on the sofa, watching the flames alternately stretch and wave. It was a beautiful memory, a powerful memory, but Otto felt it wasn't enough to sustain him after she was gone, for however many Christmases he had to bear alone.

She'd finished with the pinecone garland and now rested gratefully in the armchair. Otto went to the hall and carried in the box of tree candles he'd brought up from the cellar. Her eyes opened wide when she realized his intention. They'd only lit the candles that first year – never again. They'd become American, in this way and in a thousand others. And in their American life, they'd decorated their trees as their neighbors did, using colored lights and glittery tinsel. The only concession had been the pinecone garland. *Tannenzapfen*.

Otto attached each of the candles to the sturdiest branches with fresh wire, as the old wire had become brittle and broken. When the last candle was in place, he struck a long safety match and began lighting them one by one. Finally, he blew out the match and went to turn off the table lamps. She had moved from the chair to the sofa and sat there waiting for him. They held hands and watched the candlelight flicker off the ochre walls and ceiling. After a long while she spoke.

"You know they are female, Otto," she'd said.

Otto had sunken down on the sofa and was feeling sleepy when her words roused him. "What do you mean, *mein Schatz?*"

"*Die Tanenzapfen*, the pinecones – they are female," she said.

Otto had never considered pinecones as having a gender and wasn't sure why this information was important. It seemed that by introducing this vague botanic fact she was somehow missing the point of this moment he'd engineered, this memory-in-the-making.

He felt slightly stung.

Seeming to know his thoughts, she raised the hand that she still held to her lips, and placed a feathery kiss upon it. They had come to this land together but now she would be leaving alone, and with her would go all the love Otto knew in this world. He was desperate to build as many memories as he could in the time they had left together, trying to fill each moment with enough meaning that it would survive in his mind. It then occurred to him that, perhaps, she knew this.

"Yes, I suppose that makes sense," he answered, and squeezed her hand.

So now this new, fresh memory would hang in this room. Otto hoped it was strong enough.

A CHRISTMAS TO REMEMBER

C. W. PASS

The bells of the church tower chimed and ended in a loud clunk. The eerie noise startled the two six graders Joey and Ed as they built their snowman. While nearby a worker in the street putting up Christmas decorations walked over and asked them, "What kind of snowman are you making?"

"Well, it was going to be a he and then we decided he should be a she," replied Joey. "So why the broom and red eyes?"

Joey shrugged and looked at Ed who said, "I don't know. It just seemed right."

"Oh, she kind of reminds me of the old witch, Heady. I can't wait to see her when she's done."

"You're right. She does kind of look like her. Come back tomorrow, we should be done by then."

"I think I will. See you."

"See ya," replied the boys, as they went back to packing snow while deep in the woods outside of town lived Heady Jackals, a descendant of the witches of Salem. She was busy making her own snowmen and painting them dark green. Strange, but not-so-much for her eccentric cottage covered in sea shells, painted crimson red, and sporting a roof with a giant broom drew tourists from far and wide. This was likely a new way for her to attract tourists for business was practically nonexistent in the winter.

But in the summer, tourists flocked in droves to the picturesque town and Heady's place. They were her only source of income and she made a tidy sum from the brews and potions she sold. None of which did anything and the money was enough that she could spend the winters in Florida. But this year was different. She wasn't the happy, play-it-scary witch the tourists so loved. This year she was bitter and mean. No one knew exactly what beset the old woman, though her beloved cat, Zare, had not been seen in a very long time. Many thought the missing cat was the reason for her demeanor.

None of this mattered to Joey and Ed as Ed said to Joey, "Tomorrow is Christmas Eve.

What else do you think we need for the witch?"

"I think a cat and Heady's hat."

"My sister has a stuffed cat. Maybe we can use it, but Heady's hat, I don't think we can get that."

"Oh come on. Sure we can. I'll tell you what, tonight after dinner, we'll go to her place and get it."

"I don't think that's a good idea. Besides I'm already on Santa's naughty list. I won't get anything for Christmas if I do something else."

"Oh, you worry too much. Meet me here at six."

"Yea, okay," and the two headed home.

After a quick supper and each of them telling their parents they were going to the other's homes, the boys meet by their snow witch and Ed said with bat in hand, "I'm ready. How about you? Did you bring some protection?"

"I brought a stuffed cat."

"Nice. A lot of good that will do us, if Heady goes crazy."

"Oh, she's not crazy and she's never hurt anyone. Come on, let's go. I told my parents I'd be home by eight."

So off they went trudging through the snow. Before long they were at the edge of the woods eyeing her house lit by a single lantern swaying in the wind on the porch. It was not quite enough light to hide the boys, but dim enough that they inched slowly forward behind the trees. As they moved up, they used the snowmen as cover, but that was a mistake for in an instant the snowmen grabbed them. Somehow the ice men were alive and Ed yelled, "Run Joey run."

But it was too late. The snowmen's icy grip held them tight. Before long they were marched to Heady's door. The old rickety barn-like door opened upwards and there stood the old witch. She rubbed her hands together, which consisted of three fingers on one hand and four on the other, and then said, "So you boys thought you could get my hat, eh?"

Shivering in fear, the boys didn't answer.

"Cat got your tongue?" she laughed as she pried the stuffed cat from Joey's hands.

"Hey that's mine."

"No, it's mine, unless you want to trade the cat for you."

"Uh. No. That's okay. You can keep it."

"That's what I thought. Now what do you boys think I should do with you?"

Ed looked straight in her grass green eyes and said, "I think you should give us your hat and let us go."

Cackling she said, "You're so funny. I think I'll use you first."

"You don't scare me. My dad will crush you."

"Not a chance. He won't see the light of day after I have Santa."

Ed looked at Joey and said to Heady, "Santa? What does Santa have to do with anything?"

"You boys are not the brightest, are you? Santa has magic. Why do you think you built a witch in front of the church? You didn't think that was your idea, did you?"

"Um. It was our idea," said Ed.

"No, it was my idea. I put the thoughts in your heads."

"Okay, so if you did, then why are we here?"

"Well. I need both of you to

strengthen my powers. Zare, bless his seven lives, didn't have enough juice for my powers. But you two will do nicely. I can suck the souls right out of you and have all the power I need."

"You can't do that. We're too young to die," exclaimed Joey.

"Oh, you don't need to worry just yet. I need you to do a few chores for me first."

"We're not going to help you," said Joey and with a quick wave of her wand the boys fell into a deep sleep.

When they awoke, they were in their beds at home. Before too long, they were back at their creation, adding Heady's hat to their snow witch and painting her green. Next Ed pulled Zare from a sack. He set it on the snow witch's shoulder. All the while its eyes seemed to follow his every move.

Finished, Ed said to Joey, "What did we just do?" "We made the prettiest witch this side of Salem."

Behind them, the worker from the day before said, "You're right. It's pretty... ugly."

"No, she is pretty. Wait until tonight when she comes to life," said Joey.

Laughing, the worker replied, "You boys are dreaming. Snowmen don't come to life."

"Ah, but it's not a snowman. It's a witch and witches have powers," said Joey.

The worker smiled and went on his way as Joey said to Ed, "What next?"

"We might as well go home. Nothing's going to happen until midnight."

"Okay, I'll meet you back here," said Joey and the boys went back to their homes and fell fast asleep.

Not long before midnight, the sound of sleigh bells jingled in the air. It was Santa. The noise woke the boys. Joey snuck easily out of his house, but Ed was stopped by his father who asked, "Where do you think you're going?"

"To see Santa."

"Right? Where are you really going?"

"Um, I don't know."

"That's not an answer. You must plan on doing something."

"No. Nothing. I just wanted to see Santa."

"Is that so?"

"Well maybe... I should go back to bed."

"Wait. Come here. Let me look at your eyes."

Ed complied and his father looked deep inside his son's eyes. Being that Ed's father's ancestors were witches and warlocks, he could see things. He could see Heady through his son's eyes and knew he was under her spell.

So he told his son, "You know what, I think you should go see Santa."

"Really?"

"No. Now go back to bed."

"But?"

His father looked at him sternly and Ed turned and trudged to his room. He waited until all was quiet and then he slipped out his window and climbed down the trellis to the ground.

Quickly, he made his way to Joey and their snow witch. Standing beside them was Heady with her snowmen, while unbeknownst to Ed, his father followed and kept out of sight.

Ed's father saw Heady holding a globe in her hand. Inside were Santa and his reindeer. She rubbed her hands over the globe and peered inside as did the boys. And then she said to the boys, "See what magic can do? I have Santa and once I have your souls, I'll...."

At this point, Ed's father revealed himself and said to Heady, "Why?"

"Stay where you are."

He did and asked, "But why do you want their souls?"

"It's the only way to make my powers complete."

"Why now?"

"You know why. It is written in the Diaries of Salem, every five hundred

years, the first snow right before Christmas has magic. And the first born of a warlock has powers that can only be taken on Christmas Eve. Your Ed here has the powers I need and along with Santa's magic dust, I'll be me again."

"Not so fast, you old bag of dirt, you know I can stop you."

"Not a chance," she said and then her snowmen grabbed him.

He tried to pull loose and she cackled loudly, cracking the stained glass windows of the church causing a few shattered pieces to fall to the ground. Joey grabbed one and cut her face. The old witch screamed and waved her wand toward Joey. Instantly he was frozen like a statue. She quenched up her face and looked at Ed and his son, and then said, "You two try anything; you'll end up like him."

Ed stepped back for a moment and his father said, "Let my son go, now."

She laughed and waved her wand toward him and he was frozen, too. She smiled and turned to Ed and said, "Well, it's just you and me and then the world."

"You don't scare me."

"Maybe not. Let's see if my sister will make you feel a little less brave."

"Sister? You don't have a sister."

"Sure, I do. You made her for me. Now watch."

She laughed and shook the globe over the frozen witch. Sparkles of magic dust fell from Santa's pockets and the ice witch came to life. Her bright fire eyes burned bright in the cold night, and she let out a yell that could be heard for miles. The old cat Zare fell into the snow and Heady cackled and then said to her sister, "Are you ready to help me... take over the world?"

The icy witch looked her up and down. She laughed, got on her broom, and took off into the night sky. She circled once, twice, and on the third round she took out Heady's snowmen with a blast from her eyes. Heady scrambled for cover as the next blast came her way.

She dropped the globe and Ed - released from the grasp of the snowmen - picked it up. The icy witch circled back around and icicles flew from her broom toward Ed. He jumped behind a pile of snow and was followed by Zare.

Ed looked at the cat and said, "Git," but then the cat replied, "I can help." Astonished Ed said, "You can talk."

"Of course I can talk. All cats talk."

"But, I thought you were dead."

"Do I look dead? Cats have nine lives. I'm up to seven, so I'm good."

"Ok, so what do we do? I mean... I don't know."

"Just believe in me and we'll do fine. First, we need to set Santa and your dad free."

"Okay. So what about Joey"

"He'll have to wait. Heady has no idea what she did. She's still under the curse."

"Curse? What curse?"

"Never you mind that for now."

"So how do we set my dad and Santa free?"

"You'll have to do it."

"Me. But how?" "Let's see the globe."

Ed held the globe up, while Zare peered inside. Santa and the reindeer were tangled up. Slowly, Ed turned the globe right side up and Santa shook his head. Zare nodded and then said, "Ed, you have the powers of warlock, but only for tonight. All you need to do is close your eyes and imagine Santa and his reindeer are full size next to your father. Can you do that?"

"I will try."

Ed closed his eyes and began to concentrate. The globe started to glow and turn cloudy, but then it turned clear again. Santa and his reindeer were still inside and Ed said, "I can't do it."

"Sure you can. I'll help. Now let's try again, together."

Again, Ed closed his eyes, while Zare put his two front paws on the globe. The glass broke apart and Santa with his sleigh and reindeer were beside Ed's father. Ed opened his eyes and beside him stood a man in black garb who said, "You did good, kid."

"Who are you?"

"I am Zare."

"But you were a cat."

"I was. You broke the spell I've been under for over five hundred years. Thank you."

"I did that."

"You did. Now we must stop Heady and her sister."

"But my dad and Joey what about them?"

"Watch!"

"Ho! Ho!" bellowed Santa and with a sprinkle of Christmas magic, Ed's dad and Joey came back to life.

Joey said, "What happened?"

"When you're on the naughty list, bad things happen. You've…. Let's just say, you need to be good from now on," said Santa.

Joey nodded as, Santa hopped in his sleigh and said, "Zare take care of this. I've got to go. It's Christmas."

"Will do, Santa," and they all watched as Santa took off. But close behind, Heady's sister appeared out of nowhere. She fired a couple icicles toward Santa, who dodged them. Before she could let off another round, Heady on her broom crashed into her sister. The noise was deafening and the sisters crashed to the ground.

Quickly, the icy one got up and headed toward her sister. Fire was in her eyes. She took aim and let out a blast. Heady rolled over and was safe for the moment. In seconds, Zare was at Heady's side. He put his hands up and a mystical ball like the aura borealis appeared between his hands. He unleashed the ball of mystical magic, enveloping the ice witch.

She screamed, "It's not over. I'll get you. I'll get you all," and then she was gone. All that remained was a giant pile of snow.

Joey, Ed, and Ed's father watched in awe at the spectacle, while Heady put her head into her hands

and cried, and then said, "I'm sorry. I didn't mean to..."
And no sooner had she spoke when Santa appeared overhead with a hardy, "Ho! Ho! Ho!" He opened his bag of magical dust, which sparkled in the night and fell upon Heady. She was enveloped in the cloud and momentarily the brightness blinded everyone. As the light subsided, the old witch was gone and replaced by a younger, beautiful maiden. There was a twinkle in her eyes as she and Zare embraced. They seemed to hold onto each other forever until Ed goes, "Hey, what's the deal with you two."

At which point, Ed's father interjected, "Let them be. They can be together again."

"Again? What do you mean?"

"In the Salem Diaries, there is written of the tale of a couple of their kind cursed by the witches of Salem five hundred years ago for helping a commoner. Zare and Heady were that couple. Now they can live their lives and the events of today are in the book as well."

"So, I helped with that and you're a warlock?"

"Yes you helped and like you, I only have powers at certain times. It's all in the book."

"So when do I get the book?"

"When you're twenty-one, just like I did."

And then Joey chimed in, "So what about me?"

Zare and Heady walked up and said, "Thank you Joey. Thank all of you and Merry, Merry Christmas to all."

Joey smiled and said to Ed, "This was the best Christmas ever."

"It sure was Joey. It sure was."

"Can we do it again, next year?"

"No!" sounded Ed, Zare, and Heady in unison.

THE END

My Name is Lee

Marsha Schuman

Darrick Shoulbrun was going off to college. He had his mother's bluish eyes and his father's height. He was quite a debonair young man. Yes, Lee Shoulbrun's only son was finally eighteen and looking forward to being on his own.

"Dad, I have never asked you, was it hard to get your first job?"

Lee took a very slow, deep breath, not knowing what to tell his one and only son. Finally, he decided upon the truth, because it sounded so preposterous that he probably wouldn't believe him anyway.

"I'll share my story but you never can repeat it, deal?"

"Deal."

One day, I sat alone in my apartment not knowing what to do, where to go, or how to change my worthless life. I had, after all, applied for many jobs with countless resumes having been sent without results. I was in limbo, that wait-and-see endless time zone, where people just don't respond. HR departments would just never communicate, leaving me to wonder why I couldn't get a job. People who were no smarter than me had gotten jobs, always through connections. Our family wasn't connected.

Necessity had required me to take out endless loans that had accrued to almost two hundred thousand dollars of debt. Now, I sat in a chair and looked at the vodka and the bottle of pills on the table. I kept asking myself how I could be so young, and yet so despondent? How could it be? How could I feel this miserable when I was only in my twenties? Don't those feelings of misery, depression, and failure usually come later in life when your best-forgone plans have all gone awry?

I took one pill and washed it down with the bitter but cold vodka. Then I took another, and another, each time gulping a little more of the potent fluid, hoping to wash away my own pain. I was about to swallow the fourth Xanax when my phone started ringing. It showed Yellow Bird. I tried to regain my composure since the booze and tranquilizers hadn't yet had time to do the deed. Quickly, I answered the phone.

"Yes, this is Lee Shoulbrun."

"Oh, Mister Shoulbrun, I had thought you were a woman, with the name Lee it's often hard to ascertain."

I couldn't explain why, but it was something to do with the way the voice on the other end said Mister as if she was trying to contain her disappointment. For some weird reason, maybe it was the alcohol and tranquilizers mixing into my bloodstream, I decided to do something crazy.

"I am a Miss and not a Mister. I just have a bit of cold and always have had a deep voice."

"Well, Miss Shoulbrun, I am Evonne from HR at the Yellow Bird Company, and we found your resume to be most intriguing. Would you be able to come in for an interview tomorrow at two pm?"

"I believe I'm available at that time, can you tell me a bit about the position?"

"Um, well, I really don't know much about anything, I was just asked to have you here tomorrow at two pm."

"Fine, thank you, I'll be there."

I could barely hold my head up since the drugs had kicked in, and made me feel as if my body had run ten miles in a desert heat. Complete weakness had overtaken my senses. As a man who always tried to be the most prepared in all circumstances, I had a bottle of Syrup of Ipecac next to the vodka just in case I chickened out of dying. Quickly, barely able to hold the glass, I drank the awful-tasting syrup known to make one vomit if poison was swallowed.

My knees buckled and I fell to the floor. I had just begun to sleep when my gag reflex took over and woke me. I immediately started spewing yellow-green vomit across the floor from the Thai food I had eaten the night before. As I retched across the room, I felt as if I had thrown up my old manly self to become a more feminine Lee Shoulbrun.

"Darrick, of course, I was what a lot of women would have said, a damn handsome guy. I have always been in my own mind, a real masculine kind of a man, ready to take on challenges. You know, an athletic, sports-motivated kind of a guy. But this, it was all kind of new to me. After throwing up for what seemed like hours, I made a strong pot of coffee to remove the regurgitating vomit taste in my mouth. Quickly, I drank three cups and tried to wake up and think about the last two hours.

At first, I had been totally despondent and decided because of my huge debt that life wasn't worth living. Then, just when I counted on dying, in one of the very last moments when anything mental still made sense, I got a call about a job.

It was at one of the most prestigious technology companies in the US. I immediately went to my piles of job applications and started hunting to find which jobs I had applied for at Yellow Bird.

In the last year, I found that I had applied for technology designer, computer optimization specialist, and also an intra-technical marketing specialist, just at that company.

I couldn't figure out what made me tell the caller that I was a ... woman? Surely, it must have been the drugs. How I desperately needed that job. What would I wear? How should I speak?

Why did I do it? Was I secretly a transvestite? No, I figured it was probably a mixture of the drugs and alcohol, which had made me speak irrationally. But now what? I really needed that job, whatever it was.

I went to the thrift shop and asked a saleswoman to help buy clothing for my mom. Next, I explained that she had a broken leg, and couldn't get out of the house. Finally, I described her as quite thin and about my height, with very large feet for a woman. In fact, they were a size fourteen and extra-wide. I was looking for a conservative suit, flats, and a nice blouse. A jacket would be best to cover my flat breasts and a good-looking suit is the universal standard for both men and women. I then purchased a dark-haired wig, chin-length cut with full bangs.

Next, was the makeup. I couldn't help but think, what if I got the job? I would have to buy an entirely different wardrobe. What if I didn't get the job, should I go back and kill myself?

Yes, I, Lee Shoulbrun, was in very uncharted territory when I went to Walgreen's makeup department.

Of course, I did have two sisters, your Aunt Lucy and Aunt Marie. How could I ever forget their leaving makeup all over the bathroom counter from the time they were twelve until they were in their late teens? Then, I was so irritated by their clutter of junk thrown everywhere. But now, I was grateful for the scattered bottles of earthtone tan foundation, midnight blue eyeliner, and noir black mascaras. It all prepared me for this moment. I remembered they wouldn't leave the house without putting on their foundation and mascara. So, I knew those were necessities. Maybe the bangs would keep them looking at my eyes and the top portion of my face. It was obvious that my almost grown out beard would have to go.

I decided I'd leave the house at one fifteen to ensure that I'd be on time. I donned the wig, applied the makeup, and slipped into my newly acquired business suit. Once dressed, I turned once or twice around and looked into the mirror. What had happened to the twenty-five-year-old stud who has been captain of the basketball team and loved to row?

Well, as a woman I wasn't exactly beautiful, but I wasn't ugly either. With ambiguity and complete uncertainty about how I should walk, speak, or act, I left for the interview. On a positive note, I was so engaged with trying to be feminine that I forgot to worry about the meeting.

I pulled up at Twenty-two Park, near Bradford Street. It was an impressive building created in a Neo Revival style showing smooth lines accented by gleaming brass structures. I entered the elevator and pressed the button for the thirty-second floor. I arrived at the reception desk and announced myself.

"Hi, I'm Lee Shoulbrun. I was called yesterday by Evonne from HR for an appointment. However, she did not say with whom I was to meet."

"You have a meeting with Andrea Ulzmtat, Vice President of Technology. She is expecting you Ms. Shoulbrun. Please follow me."

With trepidation, I followed the cute petite blonde who had a tight curvaceous butt. Then, I remembered that I was supposed to be a woman. How had this happened?

"Miss Shoulbrun, nice to meet you. I'm Andrea Ulzmtat, VP of Technology here at Yellow Bird. You were asked here for a rather unusual reason. We have hundreds of qualified applicants for various technological positions, but none of them stated their hobby is rowing. I was quite surprised to read that you were part of McMillian's rowing team. Were you the only woman since I had thought it was an all-boys school?"

I tried to think fast.

"At McMillian, the coach was very fair, and he chose people based upon their ability not their gender. If you could pull an oar and move the boat well, that's all that counted." I changed the topic.

"I'm a bit surprised that my ability and interest in rowing appears to have made such an impression. I hope that you also found my graduating at the top of my class from USC helpful in obtaining this interview. I would love to show you how my extensive abilities in coding would be an asset. If I may inquire, what position do you need filled here at Yellow Bird?

I really strained to concentrate on Ms. Ulzmtat's words. Because I am a true man, I could not resist noticing her vivid blue-green eyes framed by neatly plucked eyebrows, her turned up nose and her well-formed breasts. After studying her for a few moments, I was also surprised that she had attained such a high management position when we appeared to be about the same age. My relentless thought of how I desperately needed the job, quickly forced me out of my momentary daydream.

"Ms. Shoulbrun, each year we have a work picnic with another big tech company. This year, we will share the day with Croogle, Inc. Each afternoon at noon, there is a rowing competition. Our president, Mr. Henry Ultzmtat, is upset, or should I say not pleased that we have never won in ten years. If you were hired, for a tech position you could start as an administrative supervisor. The base pay would commence at eighty thousand a year with full benefits. Could we count on you to spend much of your own time with our soon-to-be rowing team?"

I immediately answered, "Yes, that would be fantastic."

But I really had not thought the whole thing through. My legs would need to be shaved daily, as well as concealing my heavy facial stubble with thick makeup. I would have to appear to be a woman. Then, I started thinking about the workouts needed for rowing. I would continuously need to move my head forward to glide with the abdominal pull of the oars. What if the wig fell off? Oh, it was all too complicated. Why did I say Lee was a woman? But it was far too late for the die had been cast.

It was the third week in July when the interview took place. My probationary period would be over in ninety days, which would make it winter. They wouldn't start rowing until early April. I went home that night and thought about what I was going to do. I couldn't go to work every day being someone I'm not, hiding my real identity, or could I? But I needed that job. I had that two hundred thousand dollars of debt lording over me, and the default notices were closing in.

I decided that I would go to work for the next five months as the feminine Lee, and then tell everyone that I was going to have a sex change in mid-March. I was out for two weeks, and returned on April first, as *Mr. Lee Shoulbrun.* I had a lot of funny looks. It was at that time that I needed to start rowing on the Charles River. Thankfully, as Mr. Lee Shoulbrun, I was able to go out without worrying if the wig would fall off.

"Dad, you've told me some real whoppers through the years, but this has got to be one of the craziest made-up stories I've ever heard. You are just telling me this because I'm going off to college, and you want me to have a wakeup call, right?"

"Andrea, honey, tell our son how we met."

Contact the author at
mostfabulouswriter@gmail.com

Sylvester "Vess" Louis Ossman, The Banjo King

1868 (Hudson, NY) - 1923 (Fairmount, MN)
Dramatic Monologue by
Peter H. Green

Based on articles by Jim Walsh in Hobbies Magazine, September 1948 to February 1949 and an interview with Howard Weilmuenster, banjoist, May 10, 2011

*M*r. Vess L. Ossman strikes you as every inch *a man. There is grit, determination and power and his handsome good-humored features. Clean shaven, with hair waving over a high, broad forehead, eyes brown, honest and returning your gaze, frankly twinkling humor as some funny story arouses his sense of fun, a sensitive mouth and a frank, open countenance, he is one in a thousand. He talks admirably with a quick laugh throwing up his head a trifle the while. Of medium height, above rather than below the average standard, quietly dressed, you know him to be an American gentleman literally one of the best. Frankly, one more loyal or considerate, one better to deal with, one more willing to give than to receive, a shrewder, better, more cheery, more honorable as friend, comrade and fellow musician, it is impossible to mention. —Home Gordon, Editor B.M.G. (Banjo, Mandolin, Guitar) Magazine, March, 1903*

[Lead in music: Internet digital recording of original wax cylinder, "A Bunch of Rags," by Vess Ossman]

Hear that? That's how the banjo ought to be played. My name's Sylvester "Vess" Ossman. They called me "The Banjo King." I started playing the banjo when I was twelve. I became the unchallenged king, all right, from the 1890s up to the Roaring 20's—at least until that gol-durned Fred Van Eps came along.

You see, back in the 1890s the banjo was all the rage. Lots o' folks had 'em. The banjo was not only an enormously popular instrument, but it recorded so well that the banjo player's individuality and personal traits could be detected by the casual listener. Columbia Records said in their 1896 catalog, where they listed fifteen of my recordings, "Mr. Ossman is without a doubt one of the finest banjo players in the world. His records are wonderfully loud. They have all the true banjo tone." See, back in those days we recorded directly on wax cylinders. To play a record, you had to have a machine with big horn on it that would play the wax cylinder. There were no electric amplifiers and no way to duplicate the cylinders except to make more. So to make 160 records, I would have to sit down and play the song forty times with four recording machines running, while the machines inscribed the sound track on the wax. That'll fill yer afternoon, let me tell you, and it's darned good practice. Nobody could play as fast or as well as I could.

Ragtime was the rage in those days. I played a big five-string banjo, with gut strings, long before they had nylon—and could I pluck out those rags. They called me "Plunks." Some of my biggest hits were *A Bunch of Rags, St. Louis Tickle* and *Turkey in the Straw Medley,* including *Dixie, Arkansas Traveler, Sailor's Hornpipe* and *Turkey in the Straw*, which created a sensation.

I played twice for King Edward VII of England, in 1900 and 1903, and played at three magnificent halls in London—the Palace, the Tivoli and the Alhambra, where I had a wonderful reception. Everybody I came across in England appreciated the banjo. Why one London critic, a banjoist himself, once said to me that when he heard me play he felt inclined to go home and burn his banjo. I said to him, "When I hear a better player than myself, I work all the harder."

Let me tell you what makes a good musician. No doubt hard work and infinite patience form the basis of it. Practice does it: ten hours a day for three years, four hours a day, and after that, pretty nearly all year around. Scales are the foundation of music and they are the foundation of dexterity on the banjo. So let no one, teachers or pupils, neglect them.

Now Fred Van Eps and I—we had a great rivalry. People took sides: some said I was the best and others said he was. But when folks started calling him the "World's Greatest Banjo Player," that was the last straw. Heck, he admitted himself that I was his inspiration to learn to play the banjo. He learned how to play from my records. I asked him one time to do me a favor. I trusted him to take over one of my concert dates. I had this recording contract in New York City that paid very well. Then I got an offer to do a concert out here in the Midwest during that same week. So I asked Fred and a fine banjoist named Bill Bowen to do it for me. So they did the concert run for four days. I was very relieved that I could go and earn my money in New York. We were rivals, all right, but we still had a certain mutual respect.

By this time we had the electric phonograph and pressed disc records and I was on even more labels— Edison, Pathé, Victor. I formed banjo orchestras and played at the leading hotels throughout the Midwest and in New York City.

But Van Eps kept playing until he had recorded for 25 record companies. He started manufacturing electrical equipment, and then he began to make banjos. And here I was, still touring to earn my living on the vaudeville stage. In fact, that's where I died, while still on tour after a charity performance in Fairmont, Minnesota. They say Fred Van Eps even was asked by the federal government to work on the Manhattan Project, to develop a timed-release mechanism for the atomic bomb that helped us end a horrible world war. He must've been a great man. But you know what? Like the old philosopher, I say, "To be great is to be imitated." I was great long before that young whippersnapper ever came along.

I was the Banjo King.

Written for Voices of Valhalla
For more, visit: AuthorPeterGreen.com

Candles and Bells

Glenn Sartori
An altar boy in action

I became an altar boy to meet girls.
Really, you say. Well, don't judge so quickly. My motive was not as bad as you think. Number one, I was volunteering, and no matter what the reason, volunteering is a laudable undertaking. Even today, people voice the phrase "give back to the community" as if it were a battle cry. Number two, my church needed boys to serve at Mass. And number three, I was a teenager.

It was May 1953, Sunday morning, fifteen minutes before Mass was to begin.

Bob and I were the altar boys on that Sunday morning. We had been friends since kindergarten and served many Masses together. I thought this morning would be just another time on the altar.

Over our street clothes, we put on our black cassocks and white, stiff-as-a-board surplices—there was no conservation of starch at my parish. Then we had the ritualistic duty of helping dress the priest for his role as the celebrant. Fans of *Downton Abbey* might picture Bates dressing Lord Grantham. In our case, it was much less than that. Our valet service consisted in handing the priest various parts of his outfit such as the stole and the girdle. No, it's not what you think. The girdle, or more appropriately, the cincture, was a cord the priest tied around his waist after he had put on the Alb, a long-sleeved, white tunic. We were too young to reflect on that social ceremony in the spiritual world. In time, like any other ritual, it became perfunctory.

Anyway, after Bob and I assisted Father Alvin, the celebrant for the Mass, in donning his vestments, he left the sacristy for a smoke. Don't gasp—it was the 1950s.

Our next task was lighting the candles, usually a mindless undertaking, although timing was everything.

The countdown had begun. In three minutes, I would walk into the sanctuary and light the altar candles. The wall clock demanded our total attention. The tick tock of the second hand sounded like a metronome during a piano lesson.

With one minute to go, I extended the wick on the candle-lighting tool, and Bob struck a match. The wick absorbed the flame. I adjusted the length of the exposed wick and was about to leave when the pastor, Father Vincent, strode into the sacristy, his gray hair sprayed into place. Unlike Father Alvin, who seemed as if he wanted to be elsewhere, anywhere, the pastor wanted to be here, in control, in charge.

Father Vincent pointed a gnarly finger at me. "Your surplice is crooked." His voice was like a drill sergeant. I trembled as I struggled to straighten my surplice with my left hand, my right holding the lighting tool— its flaming wick quivered high above me. I started to sweat—pores perspired that never perspired before. Rivulets emanated from my pits and trickled down my sides, but I stood erect, waiting for his next complaint. It never happened. Why? He noticed Bob standing behind me. Bob wasn't going to a "regular" high school; he was going to the seminary to become a priest. Like all seminary-bound boys, Bob got a free pass. Father Vincent treated those boys special, not like the other altar boys—he acted as if we were his minions.

He flicked a smile at Bob then turned back to me. "Isn't it time to light the candles?" His voice was softer but certainly not pleasant.

"Yes, Father," I squeaked, nodding my head like puppet, and walked slowly out of the sacristy. This was not good.

I could feel Father Vincent's stare burning into my back as I lit the altar candles in the prescribed order. Oh yes—you must follow a specific sequence; there was no dispensation, just the wrath of the pastor, if you took a short cut.

The sequence was—first, the six candles on the altar, lit from right to left, and then the two candles that were astride the pulpit. (In the 1950s, the candles were on the altar because the priest said Mass with his back to the congregation.) Each altar candle succumbed to my burning wick—six lit and two to go. My spirits were high until I saw the two candleholders next to the pulpit. My pride extinguished. They had new candles, tall candles, never lit candles, and I knew it would be a difficult task to light them. I raised the lighting-tool to the sterile wick, stretching, straining and willing it to flame up. The wick refused to obey me. Sweat started up again and began to dampen my neck and forehead. My arms ached.

Glancing out into the church, I saw people meander up the aisles and sidle into the pews. Time was running out. I lowered the tool and thought that if I lengthened the wick, maybe that would help. Someone brushed my shoulder, grabbed the candleholder and tilted it to eye level. I looked up at Father Alvin as he flipped his cigarette lighter open and lit the candle. He did the same to the other one, smiled and returned to the sacristy. I extinguished the wick, stood there for a moment and wondered if Father Vincent had witnessed that event, but found only Father Alvin and Bob in the sacristy.

I sighed louder than I intended as I returned the lighting tool to its cabinet—another task accomplished in the correct order.

"Let's go, boys," Father Alvin said with a wave of his hand, and Bob and I led the priest into the sanctuary for

Sunday Mass.

Our duties during Mass were minimal—being attentive, sitting still during the sermon, bringing holy items to the priest but most importantly, checking out the girls in the congregation. That was until the consecration—the time to ring the bells.

Ringing the bells was the trickiest and most tensed-filled task during Mass. There were four golden-colored bells affixed to two-crossed bars that attached to a handle. The ringing session had to start at a precise time and end at a precise time. You guessed it—Father Vincent insisted. No bell tinkling tolerated before and after the ringing session. A steady hand was infinitely important and difficult to attain especially when Father Vincent was the celebrant. He demanded perfection, never complimented the altar boys, only criticized them.

Luckily, I had excellent bell-ringing skills... still not an easy job.

My first assignment had been at an early morning weekday Mass, never a full house, and the perfect time to hone my altar-boy skills. Paired with Greg, a popular eighth grader, he had shown me the bell-ringing trick. The trick was that you ease your hand under the bells before lifting them off the floor, thus silencing the clappers. Next, release the clappers and start ringing the bells—not too rapidly, not too slowly—the correct hand speed was key. Then when the ringing is scheduled to stop, you once again immobilize the clappers with your free hand and ease the bells to the floor.

At this Sunday Mass, my bell ringing was perfect—made easier when Father Alvin was the celebrant. He would give you a nod when to start and a nod when to stop, not like Father Vincent, who seemed to take joy in making head movements to mess up the start and stop times of the ringing.

The Mass ran smoothly after that and concluded with the song, *Be Not Afraid*, one of my favorites. As the three of us headed to the sacristy, I sang in my mind, "I go before you always. Come, follow me, and I will give you rest."

Father Alvin hastily removed his vestments as if he had a place to go—probably didn't want to meet up with the pastor. His street clothes were a light-blue tee shirt, black slacks and brown sandals. He was cool.

"Good job, boys." He pulled out a pack of cigarettes and disappeared.

After Bob and I hung the priest's vestments and our cassocks and surplices in the closet, we verified that the sacristy was in pristine condition—leave it in better condition than you found it was the mantra—then rushed out of the church.

I asked Bob, "Did you see who was at Mass?"

"Yes, I did. They smiled at us at communion."

We hurried across the church parking lot and headed to *Ann's Candy Shop*, a neighborhood-meeting place for grade-schoolers. Sue and Janet were at the Mass and regulars at the confectionary.

I beamed—being an altar boy is paying off.

For more, visit: glennsartori.com

Once I Did A Rain Dance

Deborah Hart Yemm

The soil puffs up like smoke with each foot step. As I hike through the forest each day, my legs become coated with a fine dust, more like baby powder than dirt. It has been months since a useful amount of rain has fallen. I've never seen the land this dry. Only the slightest trickle of water is flowing now in the perennial creek passing by my neglected, old farmhouse. All the leaves are turning brown. Peak fall color is still weeks away. My heart wants to make a difference because the forest feels thirsty to me and the trees look like they are dying. What can I do to bring relief to the trees?

A casual remark by a friend on the internet inspires me to learn how the Native Americans do their Rain Dance. Turns out to be very simple really - toe stomp one foot and then toe stomp the other. Touch the ground with the hand, then raise it towards the sky. Twirl around a bit like the wind bringing in clouds heavy with moisture. I am a dancer with a fondness for trees and I have swayed with them in the breeze. I want to do something for the trees, so I will do a rain dance and let my love shine through the effort.

Every morning I take a stroll down the old Bloomfield Road which parallels the creek. During the pioneer days, wagons and horses and foot travelers used this road to go from their homestead to a one-room schoolhouse or a country church or to the closest general store or even to distant railroad town. The trees along this part of the road are old with thick trunks. I cannot wrap my arms all the way around them or touch fingertips. The trees tower over me like giants.

There is a confluence where the brook which runs across the old road enters the larger creek. My husband has moved large rocks into the creek to make it easy to hop across without getting my feet wet. When I go there, if it is warm enough, I slip my shoes off. I like to stand barefoot on one of the large flat rocks in the brook. A yellow butterfly begins to make a nuisance of itself, flying about my head, even landing on my hair. I flail my arms about to send it away. It is determined. I begin to laugh. Is this the Great Spirit teaching me a rain dance of my own? My arms twirl now, as though gathering the clouds, to bring in some rain.

I like to do a Sun Salutation, when I go there in the morning. This connects me to the birds and the trees, to the earth and the sky. I raise my arms towards the sun like a large Y. I feel the energies of the sun warm my head and with my arms bring these energies down to my heart. Then, I open my arms straight out. Do not think I am being crucified. The pose feels like I am balanced between giving and receiving.

I forward fold towards the little brook which is happily making noise with the rocks below me. Sometimes I see crawdads, frogs or little fish there in the water. I feel gratitude for my connection to the Earth, Mother Gaia. In my mind, I scoop up the water. I lift the water energy towards the sky. Then, with a twist of my elbows at the heart, I pass the third-eye chakra and my arms are back above my head. I open my arms out like a flower blossoming. It feels like flying. I am the butterfly.

I intend to begin my rain dance with this ritual. I don't do this every day to create rain but what the heck? Why not use it? I will add the native footsteps I saw on the video. I don't feel any pressure for it to be a success. It's only my imagination after all. What do I have to lose?

I need a chant to call in the rain, while I dance. A memory comes from deep within. I know the smell of rain coming, even before I see a cloud in the sky. I learned to recognize that as a child growing up in the desert. Words come into my mind - "Rain smells on the breeze. Freshening rain moistens the soil. Rain soaking in like a sponge. Rain to save the color of Fall leaves. Rain is life. Life supports itself. Rain coming. Rain here and now. Happy rain wetting my skin."

Where to do my dance? The first place I considered is a bit remote. It's not that being alone in the forest scares me. I've seen a wild pig running the ridge road ahead of me before. It did not seem aggressive. I don't think it had any intention of confronting me. It only wanted to put some distance between us - quickly. I am never afraid in the forest. I've seen coyotes up close more than once and never has one turned to attack me.

I did feel fear in the forest once. I had to hike after darkness in the cold of a long January night. I left the main road to take the foot trail along the creek. I was listening to a recorded book, The Stolen Child by Keith Donohue. It is a scary story. Probably not the best choice when hiking alone in the dark. I was at the deepest point on the loop, when I heard a coyote call. He was very near. I know they have a way of encircling prey as a pack.

I turned back to the dirt road - quickly. I hurried home like a scared child. I love the forest. I wasn't going to let fear haunt me for the rest of my life. So I went back out after dark the very next night. The outcome was unremarkable. By facing my fear, I felt brave again. I still avoid repeating the experience. I try to hike while it's still daylight.

In stories about magic rituals, the practitioner often goes out in the dark. Do I really need to go out at night? Darkness has powerful symbolism - the womb in creation mythology.

OK. Going out in the dark of night, just to do a rain dance seems irrational and just plain crazy to me. I can think of no reason why I can't go and do the rain dance in the light of day. This idea is natural. "There is nothing evil about dancing or wrong about chanting in the forest." I don't want to turn this into something weirder, than the skeptic in me already feels like this idea is.

Human beings have danced and sang since the dawn of time. It doesn't matter what clothes I wear. Just the usual blue jeans and t-shirt should be good enough.

My rain dance is taking shape in my imagination. My daily ritual represents the sky and the earth. Water. I need to be near water flowing. Our brook and stream take water to the great Mississippi River and from there into the sea. Water is forever circulating. Rain is forever falling. Droughts never last forever. These are the truths I want to remember.

I know now where I will go. My daily hiking trail takes me into a steep valley. This is not the same creek that flows past my farmhouse but another stream which joins it further down, passed the big shut-in waterfall.

This other creek is less well known. I never encounter strangers there like I have at the shut-ins on the main creek. This one is very private.

I know exactly where on that brook I will dance. I have fallen in love with the peace I feel at a deep quiet pool there. A slightly slanted rock shelf dips gently into the water. I have gone skinny dipping there on very hot days. It is a beautiful spot. The water tumbles down in stages and shoots like landings on a stairway of rock outcropping. Once I spied a water snake after I had been swimming there. Right where I had mindlessly let the strong flow of falling water in that pool beat upon my head. That was seriously unsettling.

The sky is a heart-stopping beautiful clear blue on the day I decide I'm going to just do it. It is hot and humid and feels oppressive but normal for this time of year - drought or not. The trees will continue to release moisture as long as they have leaves. In response to a drought, trees drop leaves to conserve moisture. Scientists calls the release of moisture from the leaves of trees - evapo-transpiration. It is their perspiration. And that is why we often have pop-up afternoon thunderstorms on hot summer days - even when no larger, organized storm systems are moving across the countryside.

Arriving at my chosen place, the trees are swaying in the breeze. Raising my arms over my head like the crowns of trees, my body sways in harmony with them. I do my sun salutation first. When I stretch my arms into that balanced pose, I notice the breeze suddenly get stronger. Whoa. Is that nature responding to my intention?

Next I do the rain dance part along with my chant. The birds go quiet for a moment and then join me to sing for rain. I return to mountain pose. I bend to the left and then to the right, noticing the tops of trees swaying alongside me.

I finish my ritual with a Namaste.

Dark clouds are approaching from the south. Can rain happen so quickly? Like a comforting blanket, the thick heavy clouds relentlessly move in. I am happy to see them. The darkness is increasing. It is so dark now, it is like early evening after the sun has gone down. The darkness is almost complete but I can still see the surroundings clearly enough. I had better hurry home. Suddenly lightning strikes. That was too close for comfort. Home is still far away. A thundering boom startles me.

Oh my! What have I done? Really? It must be a coincidence. Only I know I did a rain dance. Otherwise, I would not think it really possible to cause a change in the weather. Logically, I know this is a common thunderstorm, even though we haven't had any rain for a very long time. When I checked the forecast a week ago, there wasn't any rain predicted.

Big drops begin to fall. I'm

going to be drenched by the time I get all the way home. At least the trees look happier now. They seem to be standing taller and their leaves appear to be uplifted to catch drops the way children stick their tongues out to taste rain.

Thankfully I finally arrive home. It is pouring buckets now.

So - what happened? Twelve inches of rain fell in only a few hours. Then rain continued for days. The ground became saturated and wind gusts blowing the storms along were so strong, trees began to be uprooted. Large 50 and 100 year old oaks and pines. Trees I hug and feel a relationship with. Trees with character. I went out into the forest after the rain finally ended to look for damage, feeling full of responsibility and guilt. I felt pain in the downed trees that still have life in their leaves or roots. In trees not entirely pulled out of the ground. The plight of the trees called my heart to do that damned rain dance. I'm sad that so many trees suffered storm damage.

It may seem silly but I do feel responsibility for what happened. Can one person dancing really affect the weather? I never want to risk doing another rain dance again. I know the outcome. The fact is, it rained hard. It seems significant somehow. A rain cloud just sat there right on top of us. A lot of rain fell in only a few hours because the cloud just wasn't moving. It just stayed put, right over us, and rained, and rained.

The weatherman did have a rational explanation. The storm that blew through here was drawing moisture from the flow of a hurricane coming out of the Gulf of Mexico. I know I wasn't responsible for that hurricane. The timing though? A cloud just sitting on top of us, after I actually did a rain dance? Plain spooky.

And this story gets worse. So much rain fell, it began to stress several pond dams upstream. Due to a dam inspection in the 1980s, we knew the homemade dams upstream were at a "high risk" of failure. Over the years, wave erosion had weakened the upper side of those dams. Trees had also grown up in the downstream side. Many of those trees had been cut above the ground to kill them but their roots remained embedded.

When the first dam broke, the increasing water volume cascaded through all 3 dams above us. The flood took a lot of forest trees downstream with it. Within the damage zone were an electric transmission line, a petroleum pipeline, a few dwellings and a church. I'm glad the flood didn't take out our farmhouse too. The land near our house opens out lower and away from it. Also, our home is built on relatively higher ground.

There is an old saying - do not to mess with Mother Nature. I don't believe the Earth needs saving by humans. I do believe humans do need to care about their impact on our planet. A day may come that we will find the Earth can no longer support us.

I know, most people would scoff at the idea of one person directly causing a change in the weather. After this experience, I'm not so certain. I don't plan to ever interfere with nature this way again. Just in case . . . I did have anything to do with it.

Wall of Remembrance

Marie Chewe-Elliott

Part 1
Trayshaun Harris, Travante Greely, Joshua Harris, Precious Doe aka Erica Michelle Green, Gina Dawn Brooks, Conner Peterson, Matthew Shepherd, Rilya Wilson, Jon Benet Ramsey, Christian Ferguson, Zariah Unique Harrison, Michael and Alex Smith, Noah, John, Paul, Luke and Mary Yates, Chandra Levy, Jessica Lunsford, Dominic Williams, Heather Kullurn, Dylan Groen, Daphne Jones, Natalee Holloway, Brandi Scales, Jamyla Bolden

Part 2, St. Louis Summer 2019
Xavier Usanga, 7, Jason Eberhart Jr., 16, Baby Doe (on Magnolia), Ien Colman, 14, Eddie Hill IV, 10, Devaun Winters, 17, Robert R.J. Dorsey, 16, Omarion D. Coleman, 16, Derrel Williams, 15, Michael Henderson Jr., 15, Myresha Cannon, 16, Charniya Keys, 11, Kennedi Powell, 3, Jasleon Johnson, 16, Joseline Eichelbereger, 11, Kristina Curry, 16, Jaylon McKenzie, Micah Stringfella, 4, Kayden Johnson, 2, Curtis Marshal, 15, Malik Moore, 17, Jurnee Thompson, 8

Epitaph
No chatter, clatter or pitter-patter
No pageant crowns
Silenced giggles and
Muffled baby sounds
No prom dates
No coming in late
No Barbies or Bratz
No bouncing balls or Tonka® trucks
Graduation caps
Animal crackers
Flashing clackers
Missing
Eclipsed youngsters
Snuffed out
Like candlelight.

Thank you to all St. Louis Writers Guild Members
Past, Present, and Future.

For a century, it is writers like you who
have made this writers' guild a success.

You have friends here!

St. Louis Writers Guid
founded in 1920

St. Louis Writers Guild Membership

Regular $45
(open to all writers)

Senior $30
(65 and over)

College Student $30
(must be currently enrolled)

Associate Memberships
High School Student $5
Middle Grade Student $5

Full member benefits listed at stlwritersguild.org

You have friends here!

100th Anniversary

St. Louis Writers Guild

Celebrating A Century of Writers

1920 ~ 2020

stlwritersguild.org

@stlwritersguild

Jessica Mathews, President
T.W. Fendley, VP of Programs and Publicity
Jamie Krakover, Treasurer
Jennifer Stolzer, Secretary
Amy Zlatic, VP of Membership
Cherie Postill, VP of Contests
Brad R. Cook, Historian

**SLWG 2019 Young Writers Collection:
When the cup turned over...**

featuring
Winners and Finalists
from the 2019 Young Writers Awards

paperback and ebook available at
amazon.com

You Are a Writer!

Written and Illustrated
by Jennifer Stolzer

Written and Illustrated by Jennifer Stolzer
voted one of the "Reader's Choice Top 5 Children's Book
Authors 2017" by the St. Louis Post-Dispatch.

Don't listen to people who say you are not a writer. You
are a writer as long as you have something to say!

All proceeds from the sales of this book go to the St. Louis
Writers Guild. Thank you for one hundred years of serving
St. Louis, and for guiding and nurturing the young writers
of the world.

Available in paperback and ebook
Amazon.com and stlwritersguild.org

Made in the USA
Monee, IL
05 March 2020